MISHAPS IN PARADISE

THE PANDEMIC

 # THE MISHAPS IN PARADISE SERIES

1. Diary of an Island Girl
2. The Pandemic

LOOK FOR MORE MISHAPS IN PARADISE COMING SOON!

Check our website for more details:
www.mishapsinparadise.com

Find us on:

MISHAPS IN PARADISE

THE PANDEMIC

EVA POLIZZE

POLIZZE BOOKS

MISHAPS IN PARADISE

THE PANDEMIC

(Book 2) First Edition

Copyright © 2023 by Eva Polizze

All rights reserved.

Interior illustrations by Eva Polizze

Character design by Olivia and Claudia Polizze

Character illustrations by Kateryna Korolova

Book design by Eva Polizze and Emily Fritz

Cover design by Goran Tovilovic

MISHAPS IN PARADISE ™ is a trademark of Polizze Books, Inc.

All rights reserved.

This is a work of fiction. Names, characters, places, and incidents are either the products of the author's imagination or are used fictitiously. Any resemblance to actual events, locales, businesses, or persons, living or dead, is entirely coincidental.

All rights reserved. No part of this book may be used or reproduced in any form or by any means without written permission from the author and publisher except in the case of brief quotations in reviews and articles.

Published in 2023 in Big Pine Key, Florida, U.S.A. by Polizze Books, Inc.

Library of Congress Control Number: 2022950149

HARDCOVER ISBN: 978-1-959739-04-3

PAPERBACK ISBN: 978-1-959739-05-0

E-BOOK ISBN: 978-1-959739-06-7

POLIZZE BOOKS

www.polizzebooks.com

TO OLIVIA AND CLAUDIA,
EVEN WITH THE WHOLE WORLD SHUT DOWN,
YOU ARE EVERYTHING I NEED.

MARCH

SATURDAY

Hey. This is Sylvia White, a kid who lives on a tropical ISLAND, where it's warm all year long.

I can't believe I have already filled up my first diary, and I'm writing my second one.

Who would have known that island life could be interesting enough to fill all those pages!

Unfortunately, my life is ruined now, and for the first time ever, I have nothing to do with it!

Last week, I was excited because my life finally made a turn for the better. After we moved to the tropics in December, I made new friends at our local island school.

Unlike my younger sister, Natalia, at first, I wasn't open to meeting new people because I had always been shy and introverted.

But the island kids turned out to be awesome, and we created quite a pack.

I was looking forward to a great summer and starting middle school in the fall.

What could possibly go wrong, right?

WHAT COULD POSSIBLY GO WRONG?

How many times have I promised myself I would never ask this **STUPID QUESTION!!**

Because every time I do, something **COMPLETELY UNIMAGINABLE HAPPENS!**

You heard me right! As my life has proven many times before, **EVERYTHING CAN GO WRONG!!**

This is just my luck!!

When I finally met cool people,

I'M NOT ALLOWED TO SEE ANYONE!

Now, when I'm itching to go outside to hang out with my new friends, they want me to stay home!!

ARE YOU KIDDING ME?

Now that I can't go anywhere, I want to go **EVERYWHERE!!**

I'm dying here!!

I will even do PE!

Just get me out of my house!!

Do you want to know what happened?

THE PANDEMIC HAPPENED!

😩

SUNDAY
Before the pandemic started last week, life was normal, people dressed normally, and everyone behaved normally.

Yes, we can question what normalcy really means—but the point is, everything was as it should be—with all the good and the bad.

You know how older people like to talk about THE GOOD OLD DAYS?

Or how they say BACK IN THE DAY when they talk about a far past?

Well, this past February was OUR generation's GOOD OLD DAYS—BACK IN THE DAY when kids were allowed to be kids!

THOSE TIMES ARE OVER!

Yeah! You heard me right!

Those GOOD OLD DAYS are over!

Right at the beginning of the calendar year, we heard about this scary, serious

CORONAVIRUS

that spread from China and infected the entire WORLD.

It was pretty quick, the way it happened.

We all heard about the virus when it was only in Asia, but nobody really found it concerning, so people did what they always do—travel EVERYWHERE.

Add globalization, hundreds of flights to and from every part of the Earth, and voilà!

Within weeks, the virus infected inhabitants of almost every country, ruining kids' lives all over the world!

Usually, I don't mind getting sick because I get an excuse to lie in bed and do absolutely nothing.

Although I like reading books, nobody bothers me about watching TV all day when I'm under the weather.

So, yes, there are advantages to being ill.

But this?

THIS IS A NIGHTMARE!

No, I'm not sick! But the whole world is!

LIKE THE ENTIRE EARTH IS SICK.

COVID-19, a.k.a. CORONAVIRUS, has infected the WORLD!

The virus spreads like wildfire. People are in hospitals, and many are dying.

Have you ever heard of social distancing?

We need to avoid everyone, and, when that isn't possible, we have to stay six feet apart from other people!

When we're around others, we're required to wear masks that cover our mouths and noses to prevent the germs from spreading.

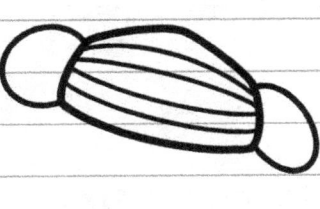

The world has gone mad! Nobody shakes hands or gives hugs and kisses.

But the worst thing is, many countries started a mandatory quarantine!

To prevent the virus from spreading, we were told to stay home for weeks on end.

We were advised against any contact with other humans, and all events were canceled.

People are not allowed to congregate anywhere!

Apart from some essential businesses, everything closed down!

I saw on the news that even

NEW YORK CITY

turned into a ghost town!

NO SCHOOLS!!

NO RESTAURANTS!!

NO MOVIE THEATERS!!

NO PLAYGROUNDS!!

NO AMUSEMENT PARKS!!

NO HANGING OUT WITH FRIENDS!!

NO TOUCHING!!

NO SOCIALIZATION!!

HOW IS A KID SUPPOSED TO FUNCTION IN CONDITIONS LIKE THESE?

When we moved to the tropics a few months ago, Natalia and I started going to the local island school with elementary and middle school in one building.

Although I am in fifth grade, and my sister is in second grade, we will both go to the same school for the next three years.

But, as soon as the quarantine started, schools ALL OVER THE WORLD closed down, and kids were told they wouldn't return to their classrooms this year.

Teachers needed extra time to figure out how to do virtual lessons and plan how to teach kids online, so students got more time off school.

You would think all the kids are happy about such a break, right?

WRONG!

We are literally not allowed to leave our houses!

It turns out being stuck at home with your family for twenty-four hours a day, every day, isn't fun.

When schools started virtual classes, parents had a choice to have their kids do online lessons prepared by the teachers from their kids' schools or homeschool kids themselves.

"What would you prefer," Mom asked us, "virtual classes from your island school or homeschool?"

I can't believe I'm saying it, but I would rather go to school than stay home for months.

But . . . if I can avoid homework, tests, and all that stress, I will let Mom be our teacher. How bad can it be, right?

So, we both said, "HOMESCHOOL!"

Mom nodded and said, "I don't want you to sit in front of the computer for hours, so I will homeschool you until the pandemic is over."

"Really, and you would do that for us?" I asked in disbelief.

"Yes, I would love to!" Mom replied. "Until schools open again."

I don't have to tell you how we reacted, I hope.

YAY!!!!!!!

I was thinking:

NO MORE STRESS!!

NO MORE BULLIES!!

NO MORE TESTS!!

NO MORE HOMEWORK!!

"Why don't you write another diary, Sylvia?" Mom suggested when we started schooling at home.

Fine! It's not like I have anything better to do during this lockdown!

Besides, writing takes my mind off things I can't control.

LIKE THIS STUPID PANDEMIC!

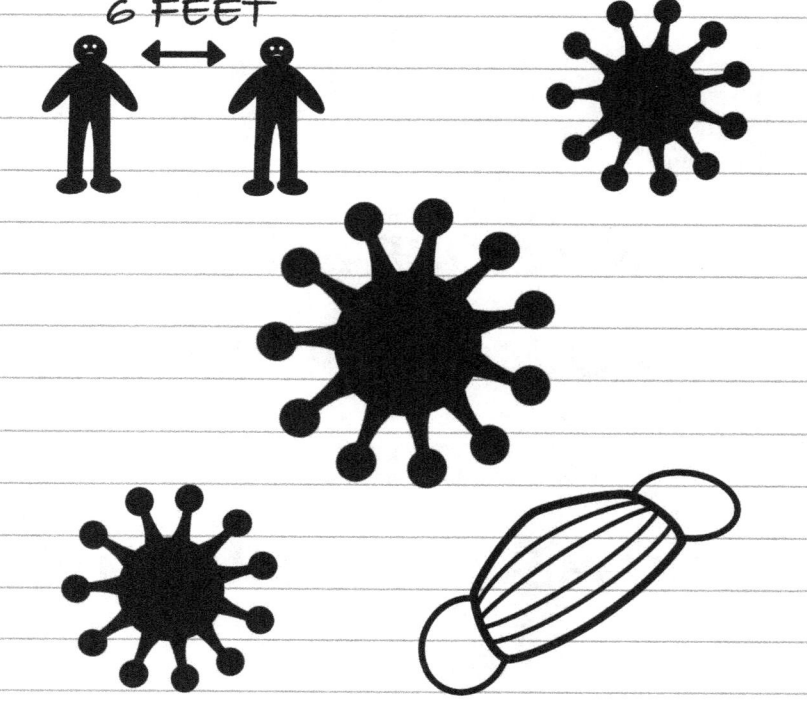

APRIL

APRIL FOOLS' DAY

Today, when I woke up, I really believed they would tell us on TV that this pandemic was ONE BIG JOKE on April Fools' Day.

We would all have a good laugh, and life would return to normal.

Instead, things got REALLY BAD!

As soon as the politicians told us to STAY AT HOME for weeks on end, people panicked and rushed to food stores like crazy.

All perishable food was cleared from the stores, and now everyone fears starvation more than the virus!

Which is not funny. Even on April Fools' Day.

Mom ordered dry and canned food online just to make sure we could survive.

I had never seen canned ham before, and trust me, I don't want to know what it tastes like, either.

Today, Dad showed us this movie—*Cast Away* with Tom Hanks—about a man stranded on a desert island who had to learn how to survive without civilization for years.

It was hard to watch, so I hope to see food arriving in stores soon because I'm NOT looking forward to drinking the nasty water from coconuts and eating bugs or weird plants.

In case we got COVID, Mom stocked up on medicine but couldn't get any cleaning supplies. And no hand soaps or sanitizers were available!

SERIOUSLY?

And just when I thought things couldn't get any worse, the entire country ran out of toilet paper!!

At first, I thought Mom was playing a prank on me on April Fools' Day! I even cracked up when she told me.

But it turned out to be 100% true!!

OUR COUNTRY RAN OUT OF TOILET PAPER!!

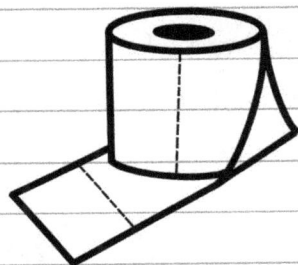

Now, can someone please explain to me why people worry about their BUTTS more than their health??

I mean, **COME ON!**

There is plenty of medicine in the stores but not a single roll of toilet paper on the shelves!

15

I don't know what people are thinking.

"HEY, WE MAY DIE, BUT AT LEAST OUR BUTTS WILL BE CLEAN!"

And we can't substitute toilet paper with something else because paper towels, paper napkins, and tissues are all GONE, too!

ARE YOU KIDDING ME?

I imagined the end of the world completely differently:

1. UFO creatures from another planet taking over Earth

2. Fires, hurricanes, tornadoes, and volcano eruptions destroying everything

3. Countries bombing each other until nothing is left

But I'd never imagined a virus would take us all.

Instead of looking like fierce soldiers or heroes fighting to survive, we might die in our pajamas, watching TV and holding on to our last toilet paper roll for dear life.

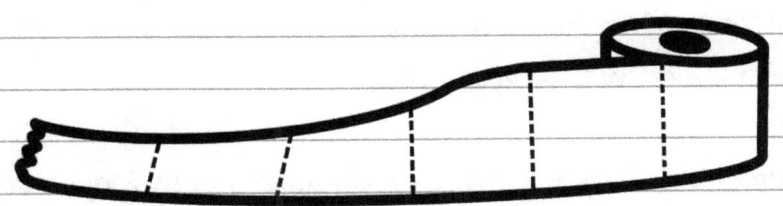

TUESDAY

Now that toilet paper is no longer available, I am terrified we will have to drag our butts across the lawn like dogs.

Whenever I see a dog doing it, I say to myself, "Yep! That will be us soon!"

Mom says we don't have to worry about such things because we have those fancy toilets with bidets.

After doing your business in the toilet, a special wand comes up and cleans your butt with a stream of warm water.

I haven't yet used the cleaning feature, but when we run out of toilet paper at home, trust me, I'M ON IT!

At first, when Mom wanted to install such expensive toilets, Dad was opposed to it.

Dad is old-fashioned and rarely agrees with Mom about technology in our house.

He said it was crazy to spend so much money on a toilet.

But Mom pressed Dad to purchase the new fancy toilets, so we got them after Christmas.

Now that stores have run out of toilet paper, Mom is walking happily around the house, saying, "And who is crazy now?"

So, I'm sure Dad is glad he listened to Mom, although he will never admit it.

But not everyone is as lucky as my family.

People started using mismatched socks as toilet paper!

SOCKS!

Well, I'm not gonna do that!

It's unfair that some people bought hundreds of rolls of toilet paper while the rest of the community has to wipe their butts with socks.

That just goes to show you how selfish some people are.

Toilet paper is so scarce that it has almost become our currency.

Whoever hoarded extra rolls can now buy things and pay with the toilet paper!

So, today, my eight-year-old sister, Natalia, and I decided to open a toilet paper-making business and use tough times to strike it rich.

First, we gathered all the empty toilet paper rolls.

Then, we collected all our drawings from sketchbooks and crinkled them until they were soft.

We cut them into rectangular shapes and glued all the pieces together to make one HUGE roll of toilet paper.

When we made twenty rolls, we put them on a small table outside of our gate with a tip jar.

And you will never believe it—those things sold like cupcakes!

So, when I become a millionaire in the future, now you know when my business skills started.

WEDNESDAY

I'll be honest with you—not everything is terrible with this pandemic.

For starters, if you're a lazy person who likes to sit on a couch and do absolutely nothing (unless watching TV all day counts for something), then the pandemic is pure heaven for you.

Now we are REQUIRED to stay home and do nothing.

Let me repeat that,

WE ARE REQUIRED TO STAY HOME AND DO NOTHING.

And by doing NOTHING, you are considered a HERO, saving the world.

This kind of thinking suits me very well!

I don't get why Mom can't understand this thinking when it's us playing online games all day long, though.

"Go outside and play on the swings with your sister," Mom keeps asking.

"Mom," I remind her, "it's not responsible to be outside. That's what they say on TV."

But Mom doesn't want to hear it. "You're safe playing on our swings in our backyard."

As you can see, when you live with your parents, it's hard to save the world.

☹

Clearly, not everyone is upset about the pandemic.

While I am dying to go places, Mom seems perfectly fine with the entire world being shut down.

She says it's a great opportunity for our family to reconnect and spend quality time together at home.

But I tell her that staying locked up with my sister is just making things worse.

Unlike me, Natalia is a social butterfly.

If you disconnect her from the world, she tends to freak out, throw tantrums, and completely hog everyone for attention.

Which means—mostly me.

I'm not a hugger-kisser kind of girl, so that is a major problem for me.

Although I like the idea of doing nothing to save the world, I'm not crazy about being stuck with my sister for months on end with NO BREAK at all.

Don't get me wrong—I love my sibling MOST OF THE TIME. But she can really drive me crazy sometimes!

She loves dress-ups, so she changes into different outfits every other hour and parades in the living room for us to applaud her fashion style.

She constantly hogs the TV to watch her annoying shows, and I need to ask her to turn it down like twenty times!

She spends the afternoons talking to her friends on the phone, which means the house is never quiet!

I don't know how I will ever get any peace around here!

And what's worse, I catch her sneaking into my room and taking my art supplies! Now that we are stuck together every day, we bicker all the time.

As you can see, I enjoy being alone, and I like my space.

When it comes down to it, I'm similar to Mom. She doesn't meet with people often and doesn't look for friends.

She says she prefers to use her time and energy on my sister and me because we are her whole world.

This is why she doesn't mind the mandatory social distancing because she says she has everything she needs right here.

Without the news on TV, I don't even think Mom would have noticed that quarantine happened.

But then again, she probably would because our business suffers during this lockdown.

My parents own vacation homes, which they rent to people weekly. Mom oversees the bookings online, which is why she can be with us at home during the pandemic.

Dad used to be a carpenter, and he often goes to the vacation homes to fix things or completely renovate bathrooms and kitchens. He doesn't do everything alone; he hires a crew to help him.

But during the quarantine, all our bookings are getting canceled, and we need to return everyone's deposits, which means we have to live on our savings.

Now Mom and Dad are home together more than ever before.

Dad started enjoying this freedom by fishing or watching TV, which doesn't make Mom very happy.

She says she doesn't like the idea of everyone doing nothing to save the world.

Because we have a pool in the backyard, a trampoline, swings, and a circular driveway where we can ride our scooters, Mom asks us to be active all day to compensate for not doing any sports.

Like doing sports would be something I would ever miss.

😂

I don't like PE classes and team sports, so being FORCED to stay six feet away from everyone suits me very well.

THURSDAY

Remember how excited I was when Mom told us she would homeschool my sister and me during the pandemic?

Well, I'm not happy about it anymore!

I will be honest with you—I imagined homeschooling as an easy-cheesy education.

I really thought I had scored this time!

How bad could this be, right?

I pictured Mom doing laundry and vacuuming carpets while I sat with my tablet, creating different setups on BUILDING WORLDS, my favorite online game.

Don't get me wrong—I knew I would have to do something—read a book, solve some math problems, maybe even do a science project.

I thought Mom would give me homework-like assignments; I'd complete them in an hour and then be done for the day—ready to hang out with my online friends from the BUILDING WORLDS game.

OH, HOW WRONG I WAS!

Today, I started to worry when a delivery truck pulled up in front of our house and unloaded lots of boxes on our doorstep.

Mom was so excited and opened them right away.

When I peeked inside the boxes, it shocked me to see so many books!

"What's that, Mom?" I asked her.

"Your and your sister's curriculums, sweetheart. Plus, all the history and science books we'll read," she said with joy.

"Why so many? Are these all the books I'll need until I go to college?"

"No, don't be silly! It's just for this year."

WHAAAAT?

I hadn't read that many books in all the past school years combined!

HELP!!

MONDAY

As it turns out, Mom loves teaching!

Like serious teaching!

What does that mean to me?

LIVING WITH A SCHOOL-OBSESSED MOTHER-TEACHER EVERY DAY!

She wants to teach us EVERYTHING!

I don't need to know EVERYTHING!!

I just need the basics, and I'll be fine!

But Mom doesn't get it!

She says she has all this responsibility now to teach us everything, and if we don't know it all, she will look bad in everyone's eyes!

Why does she worry about what everybody thinks?

She should be happy that we don't have to do homework, school shopping, outfit shopping, or study for tests!

She doesn't have to prepare our lunches, deal with the teachers, or volunteer at school!

She should be happy that so many jobs went away!

Today, Mom designated one room in the house as a classroom.

On the wall are many posters with all kinds of important information and maps.

Some of them freak me out because I don't like to be surrounded by body parts, human organs, a skeleton, or the inside of a cell.

A comfortable sofa sits across from our desks for reading time. In the closet, we have tons of school supplies, art projects, and games.

I especially like our huge smart TV! We are supposed to watch interesting documentaries, but, in reality, that's where our games are plugged in.

Because our new classroom is where we will play our games, it will be our favorite room in the house for sure!

😉

But my sister has a problem with the gigantic skeleton Mom put in the corner.

Natalia and I named him Henry, so now Henry stares at us all day long while we do classes or play games.

When my sister first saw him, she complained to Mom, "I understand you want me to know the difference between a femur and a tibia, but . . . do I need to stare at the skeleton every day to remember the names of our bones?"

What's worse, Mom couldn't afford one of those educational models, so she bought a Halloween skeleton, which means Henry has those blinking red eyes that give Natalia some serious chills.

When Mom laughed at my sister's reaction, Natalia said, "If I can't focus during lessons, know it's Henry's fault."

Let's see how this homeschooling will go. It could be comical.

TUESDAY

"Mom, how will I know if I have coronavirus?" I asked this morning while we ate breakfast.

"Some people don't have any symptoms, but those who get sick complain about fatigue, muscle pains, chest pains, fever, dry cough, difficulty breathing, plus loss of taste and smell," Mom said.

"You mean they can't taste their food?" Natalia asked.

Mom nodded. "And they can't smell it, either."

"It's a nasty disease," Dad added. "It's best to avoid it."

"Especially since they insert a swab stick so deep into your nostrils to test you that . . . it touches your brain!" I said.

"They do?" Natalia asked in disbelief.

I nodded. "Yes! That's what I heard on TV."

"I never want to get this stupid virus!" Natalia said with tears in her eyes.

Me either!

The hardest part of the pandemic is wearing masks and avoiding touching our faces so we don't transfer germs to our mouths.

It seems pretty easy, yet it's a nightmare for me. I never realized how much I love touching my face!

So, when you see me one day swarming my hands in front of my face, don't think bugs are attacking me—it's me trying to resist touching my cheeks.

I miss the days when I could be outside, hanging out with my new friends without masks or fear of getting a virus.

This afternoon, I met online with my closest friends, Alex, Grace, and Tracy, and we connected the video call with all four of us. It was so good to see them on the screen.

Alex is from our island school, and he is in the same grade as me. We used to have PE classes and art workshops at the Art Club together. He always makes me laugh and treats me like I'm important in his life.

On Valentine's Day, he gave me a friendship ring, which I wear every day and cherish very much.

Now, when we are not allowed to see each other, we often talk on the phone or chat online on our tablets.

Grace is from Alex's classroom, and she became a good friend of mine as well.

We hung out a few times before the pandemic happened, and we had so many plans for this summer!

Now phone calls and online chats are all we've got.

Tracy is from my classroom, and we sort of became best friends. Unlike me, she is more outspoken in front of other kids, and usually, she thinks on the bright side.

We also chat online, but it is not the same to see each other on-screen. I would rather see her in person!

All three of my friends do virtual classes from our island school. None of my friends' moms wanted to be responsible for their children's education on their own.

Should I be worried about my education, now that it is in my mom's hands?

Anyway, I was thrilled when I saw everyone on the screen TOGETHER.

"I cannot believe this is happening!" Grace said. "I was so looking forward to spending more time with you guys, and now it seems like it will be months before we can comfortably hang out!"

"I know! This virus sucks!" Alex said. "We had so many plans for the spring and summer! And I miss doing sports during PE classes."

"I don't miss PE; I just miss you all," I added.

"You should see how difficult it is to learn on the computer," Tracy said. "Sometimes, the online platform crashes, half of the kids don't have working microphones, and we often can't connect with the teacher at all. It's one BIG MAYHEM!"

I made a sad face. "Sorry to hear that."

Alex sighed. "So, when technical difficulties occur, the teachers send us all the classwork and homework to do at home."

"But they try," Grace added. "They really try to make it work. It's just that nobody enjoys staring at the screen for hours."

"Unless we play online games!" I said.

Everyone burst out laughing. "So true!" Alex said.

Tracy sighed. "I can't believe I worried about my looks for middle school and had my hair dyed and cut in a fashionable style—all for nothing! Nobody can see my changed appearance, and by the time they will ever allow us to go back to school, I will LOOK EXACTLY THE SAME as I did in elementary school!"

Tracy and I each had a goal for middle school.

She wanted a brand-new look, which resulted in unsuccessful hair coloring that she needed to have corrected in a professional salon.

Now Tracy has short, lighter brown, curly hair, which is the exact opposite of mine—long, blond, and straight.

My goal was to earn money on my own and do something with it that was middle school worthy.

I achieved it by doing chores around the house and earning an allowance, which I donated to the local Marine Research Center before the pandemic started.

I was supposed to volunteer my time to help with dolphins and sea lions that live there, but the pandemic ruined all those plans!

"On the other hand," I said, "my middle school plan is still going strong. I keep leaving toilet paper made of our drawings on a table outside, and people leave me some coins for it every day."

"What are you going to do with your tips?" Tracy asked.

"I'm sure I will come up with something," I told her, wondering the same thing myself.

"I want this pandemic to be over," Grace said, and Alex nodded.

"I can't wait until our parents allow us to meet. In the meantime, let's keep in touch online, okay?" I said.

They promised to call and text as much as possible, and then we ended the call.

I really hope this pandemic ends very soon!

MAY

SATURDAY

This pandemic is making everyone eat like crazy! That's what I heard on TV.

People are bored out of their minds, so they eat and eat and eat, rapidly putting on weight.

One thing I cannot understand—how come they have so much food if all the stores are still practically empty?

Wait a second! That explains it! They're the ones who hoarded the food!

They were supposed to stay home, avoid mass gatherings, and follow social distancing rules, but instead, they all rushed to the store like crazy maniacs, spreading the virus among themselves.

Well, now I don't care if they get huge bellies after all that!

I'll never forget those empty shelves in the stores.

Today, Mom took us to the local food store.

She made us wear masks and gloves. We had to wear hoodies to cover our heads and long trousers.

Mom didn't want to see any exposed skin, so she made us wear those plastic construction glasses, too. We looked ridiculous!

When we entered the store, Mom pointed to empty shelves. "I've never seen anything like this."

It looked like an **APOCALYPSE!**

There was barely any food, only some weird-looking things in cans.

But I did notice the vegan section was completely full.

I guess meat eaters would prefer to die of starvation than eat a plant-based diet.

There is this teenager who works in our local food store. I don't know his name, so I call him THE DUDE.

Of all the people I would hope to see during the pandemic, it wouldn't be him!

He despises my sister and me.

His job is to return carts from the parking lot to the store.

And that would be fine if he wasn't the one who constantly had an eye out for us.

You see, the store has those little carts for kids with tall flags so children can accompany their parents while food shopping and be a part of the entire event.

SO, THE LITTLE CARTS ARE FOR KIDS!

But what THE DUDE doesn't like about us using them is that we RIDE them.

We step on the bottom rail, push ourselves with the other foot, and zoom between aisles.

Mom doesn't know about it because we always make her believe we are shopping for our favorite cereal and snacks, so she lets us roam the store freely.

But THE DUDE knows about it! And he chases us the moment he sees Natalia and me on the carts.

If he didn't chase us, we probably wouldn't speed the way we do, but he leaves us no choice.

So, when we entered the store today, I was glad we wore our face masks.

With the hood over our heads and plastic glasses on our noses, we were practically unrecognizable.

The store was empty—maybe only ten people shopping—so Natalia and I rode the shopping carts again and made use of the empty aisles.

However, at some point, Natalia accidentally crashed into a boy in one of the aisles, and she hit the shelves.

Boxes of cereal fell on the boy, who ended up on the floor.

And you will never believe who it was!

MAX GUNOV! A bully from Natalia's classroom!

Max Gunov is a troublemaker who calls kids all kinds of names, fights boys in the hallways, and steals their things for fun.

A few weeks ago, my sister recorded his behavior on her cell phone and reported him to the teacher, which resulted in their big fight on the playground, where Natalia bit his hand!

So, you can imagine the shock on Natalia's face when she saw him without any teachers around to protect her.

When Max got up from the floor, cereal boxes were scattered everywhere. I thought Natalia would put them back on the shelves, but instead, she took off on the little cart instantly.

Then, I saw THE DUDE walking in our direction, so I followed her as well.

I suspect Max thought it was an excellent opportunity for revenge on Natalia because he quickly got up and charged at us!

We maintained a steady speed, chasing one another like crazy.

I truly believed the store employees would like to hear kids' laughter in such apocalyptic times, but I was wrong.

As soon as THE DUDE saw us, he grabbed a microphone and announced on the speakers:

"SECURITY, PLEASE REMOVE THE TWO BRATS RIDING ON THE SHOPPING CARTS IMMEDIATELY!"

Brats? Seriously?

I didn't want to wait for some guy to grab me while this virus was going on. What if he coughed on me?

So, we ran out of the store before anyone could approach us, leaving Max Gunov behind with his parents.

Mom was disappointed with our behavior and grounded us from electronics for two days.

I feel like I should hide the fact that I LOVE my tablet and cell phone from Mom because she uses this knowledge against me ALL THE TIME!

SUNDAY

Mom says that from now on, she will be ordering food from a company that shops for people and delivers the groceries to their houses.

She says it's no longer safe to be around people in the stores during the pandemic because of the virus.

You would think I am happy not to see THE DUDE anymore.

No other kids live in our neighborhood, but unfortunately, THE DUDE lives on our street, so we bump into him quite often.

He rides his skateboard, spitting all over the street, which drives me crazy!

Whenever I'm outside, I think about his gross saliva all over the place, and I walk in zigzags to avoid stepping into it.

GROSS!

THE DUDE is really fast on his skateboard, so I need to be careful. I don't want him running into me!

Usually, though, he just says, "Get lost," and passes me by.

As you can tell by now, THE DUDE and I aren't fond of each other.

But don't worry, I know how to fix his boots.

This morning, I was picking up mail from our mailbox when there he was, riding on his skateboard, a little too close for comfort.

I didn't want to catch his germs and his weirdness that might come with them, so I yelled, "Stay away from me! Six feet apart, Dude, six feet!"

Any other time, Mom would say it's rude to speak like this.

But not during the pandemic! I'm just doing my best to save humanity! Hehehehe... (That's what my sneaky, evil laugh sounds like.)

Unfortunately, THE DUDE is never shaken up about me, so he came even closer.

So, I put my hand on my head and coughed, pretending I was sick. "I don't feel well..." I said with a groggy voice.

That did the trick—he backed up immediately.

Like I said, not everything is terrible about this pandemic.

The only thing is, nowadays, when you sneeze around people, they no longer tell you, "Bless you."

They just give you the evil eye and walk far away from you.

I'm glad we don't have to go to the food store anymore because dressing like an Eskimo on a tropical island isn't my thing.

Everyone in the store dresses like astronauts—all covered up, so nobody is recognizable.

My worst fear is that I would follow the wrong family and end up going home with them!

Can you imagine?

And since I often play on my phone when I am in the car, then walk straight to my room and continue with my game, I wonder how long it would take me to realize I was at someone else's house with a strange family?

WEDNESDAY

Today, Alex and I texted for a while, making me miss my friend even more!

> **A:** I miss PE classes.

> **S:** I don't miss PE at all.

A: Fine. Then, I miss hanging out with you.

My cheeks flushed, and I was glad he couldn't see it.

S: This virus sucks.

A: Totally! This pandemic killed all my plans.

S: What plans?

A: Chilling with you at the pool this summer.

S: And snorkeling together.

A: And going to the beach together.

S: Eating six different scoops of ice cream while you taste my flavors and I taste yours.

A: Sharing a milkshake together.

S: Going on a field trip with you.

A: Counting stars at night.

S: Yeah, that would be nice!

Because we live on an island, away from big cities, we can clearly see the stars on calm nights.

 Have a great day!

You too!

If someone told me six months ago that I would be begging to go to PE classes in May, I would ask him to examine his head.

SATURDAY

Mom says I shouldn't complain about being quarantined on a tropical island because many people would switch places with me in a heartbeat.

She says we live in paradise, and tourists from all over the world come here to relax and escape from the problems of everyday life.

That may be true, but when you are only eleven years old, you need large cities with all kinds of attractions to entertain you.

All our neighbors are elderly, so Natalia and I are the only kids on our street, if you don't count THE DUDE.

Which means we are doomed.

Most of the time, watching the wild animals in our backyard is the only entertainment we get.

Because we have a waterfront property with our own beach and a private pier, we often see dolphins swimming by or playfully jumping in and out of the water.

Large iguanas bask in the sun on the rocks that line the beach, bopping their heads up and down.

Blue land crabs dig holes all over Mom's garden and scurry away SIDEWAYS every time they see me.

Small snakes wind through the mulch between the plants, and tiny lizards climb the palm trees.

When we are outside, Natalia and I need to be careful NOT to get hit by falling coconuts and massive palm fronds—both can knock you out cold!

May has brought intense humidity, so it takes only a few minutes outside to feel like you are in a sauna.

But today, something amazing happened when Natalia and I tried to occupy ourselves WITHOUT electronics in our backyard.

We sat on the pier, sipping on fruity drinks, when two massive manatees appeared in the water in front of us.

The mammals looked straight at us as if trying to say hello.

Although I had learned about them at the island school during marine biology, I have never seen one in person until now.

"Aww! I love them!" my sister said, mesmerized by the animals.

"Do you know that the legends about mermaids started after sailors saw the tails of manatees in the ocean?" I said to Natalia, remembering a lesson from school. "They believed their floppy tails belonged to women who were half fish."

"No way!" my sister said.

I nodded. "Yes. And because they heard manatees' high-pitched sounds, they thought the mermaids were singing."

Natalia looked down at the creatures swimming underneath our feet and smiled. "Well, they may not have gorgeous long hair like we imagine mermaids do, but they are still beautiful."

We watched the manatees come up for air several times, then munch on the seagrass that grows under our pier.

"I guess living in the islands has its benefits. We get to hang out with some amazing animals, don't we?" I said.

Natalia nodded.

When the manatees slowly swam away, my sister got up and undressed to her bathing suit.

"The last one in the ocean is a rotten egg!" she said and jumped into the water.

I didn't even bother to remove my clothes. I followed her, and we started splashing each other, laughing.

Maybe Mom is right—it isn't all that bad to be stuck on an island during the pandemic.

Thank goodness the island is not deserted. Can you imagine?

MONDAY

This afternoon, Tracy and I met online and saw each other on the screen.

Tracy tells me online school is awful and that I'm lucky to be homeschooled by my mom.

She needs to get up early and log in to the virtual classroom, where she sees the teacher and some of her classmates.

But because it's hard on everyone's eyes to stare at the computer screen for hours, the teachers send them lots of instructions on the internet and give them tons of homework.

It's hard for her to learn everything, and her parents are frustrated because they are practically teachers now.

And they say it's almost impossible to keep the entire house quiet when the class is live because people have babies, dogs, and business phone calls to deal with.

I'm just glad my mom was willing to teach us because I don't think I would do well with such a virtual setup.

"So, how are you doing?" she asked.

"Saving the world," I said and smiled.

Tracy burst out laughing. "Does your mom allow you to do nothing?"

"Not a chance! She does lessons even when I'm sick in bed."

"You never told me what your homeschooling looks like," she said. "Does it feel like you are on vacation all the time?"

"NOT AT ALL!!" I told her. "My mom tortures us!"

Well, it's true!

I explained to her what school at home is like.

So, this is the drill. Mom makes us read every morning, and then we answer questions about what we have read.

All the articles she gives us have questions that follow, and we need to mark the correct answers.

Then Mom teaches us about grammar, and we do worksheets to practice what we've just learned.

Later, we do math, and Mom doesn't give me any slack. I need to do as much as I did at school!

☹

Math takes me a long time, so Mom sits with me, watching my every move.

Forget about drawing in the corner of the book like I did at school!

Every time I try to sketch something in the book, she stops me and gives me this lecture about how I should appreciate having brand-new books.

How she, as a child, always had used books, all scribbled over, with bent corners.

How lucky I am!

After math, we have lunch, and that's my favorite time of the day because Mom cooks for us whatever we want (if it isn't a sugary meal, of course).

She lets us do what we like, which means we either watch TV or play online games on our tablets. Another homeschooling perk!

When we are done with our lunch break—which often lasts an hour—it's time for science (biology, Earth science, physics, chemistry), social studies (history, civics, economy), geography, or Spanish.

We do one of those every day.

This is when Mom brings one of those books from the boxes she had ordered, and she reads to us, then gives us a lecture about the topic.

Then I must read a chapter describing that topic and answer questions about it.

If you think I have it hard, my sister has it even harder!

Mom doesn't believe in keeping my sister away while we do fifth-grade science and social studies.

She teaches the same difficult stuff to the second grader!

I can't even imagine how this poor child can understand anything, but Natalia always makes everything look easy.

This is when it gets hard for me because I can't ever get away with daydreaming like I used to at regular school.

Forget about looking through a window or writing notes to a friend—my mom stops reading the second my thoughts drift off, and she tells me to pay attention. Like twenty times!

Mom is always watching, and all her attention is on me!

AND THEN, SHE GIVES US TESTS!

"You wouldn't fail your own child, would you?" I asked her once, hoping I wouldn't have to do much studying.

"You will do tests until you get it right, all on your own," she replied.

WELL, THAT'S NOT FAIR!

At least at school, when you make mistakes on the tests, you never really know about it because the tests are delivered to the parents, and you never see them again.

But my mom is all about practical teaching, and every mistake we make needs to be corrected, and often we do things twice!

I came to the conclusion that it's easier just to study for her tests so we don't need to review them again and again!

Often, when Mom focuses on Natalia's reading and math, I take longer breaks to the bathroom or the kitchen, where I grab a snack or two.

Mom complains I take too long to complete the tasks she gives me.

But when your teacher is your mom, it's hard to find that sense of urgency, if you know what I mean.

So, as you can probably tell, unfortunately, I can't get away with anything at home. Mom knows me so well that she predicts my every move.

I can't even get in trouble because she is with me all the time.

And what's worse, I never get to call in sick!

The other day, I was under the weather, so Mom gave me medicine and told me to lie in bed.

But instead of letting me watch TV all day like she used to when I attended regular school, she did lessons with me in front of my bed!

"You know, I don't feel sorry for you," Tracy said when I explained our homeschooling. "No homework, no grades, and no standardized tests . . . please, you have it made!"

She does have a point.

She said she couldn't talk for much longer because, unlike me, she had tons of homework to do and had to study for a geography test.

I feel bad for Tracy because all of her free time is sucked up by schoolwork while I have plenty of time to do whatever I want.

Like I said, not everything is terrible about this pandemic.

WEDNESDAY

Today, we had a biology lesson on the cardiovascular system in our bodies, and Mom almost fainted.

She talked about the blood circulating in the veins and arteries, explaining the functions of red and white blood cells and the platelets.

While pointing to vivid photos on the TV screen, she became pale and had to lie down on the sofa.

"Mommy!" Natalia screamed. "Are you okay?"

"I'm weak..." she murmured.

"Why? What happened?" I asked, puzzled.

"The blood... I can't look at the blood..."

Natalia and I burst out laughing because none of us gets affected by the blood.

"It doesn't bother us," I said.

Mom smiled. "That's good. That means you both can become doctors. As you can see, I can't handle it."

So, although today's lesson ended mid-sentence, I know Mom won't let us keep saving the world by doing nothing all day long.

The lesson will resume tomorrow.

Ugh.

☹

FRIDAY

Many people are not happy with the pandemic.

All hair and nail salons shut down, and women all over the world started to panic.

Apparently, when you're a grown-up, you need those places to look presentable.

I don't know much about it because Mom tells me I'm blessed with natural beauty.

But I noticed that since all the salons closed, nobody posts photos on social media or sends us cards with family pictures anymore.

I guess they all look like cavemen by now—women with broken, unfiled nails, long hair with gray roots and split ends, and men with overgrown beards.

I really hope this pandemic ends soon because if it gets worse and all the kids end up looking like the first people on Earth, then I feel sorry for our school pictures.

After two months of staying home and doing virtual school for weeks now, many kids have had enough of staying locked up at home with their families, and they are begging to return to their regular schools.

Many parents admit homeschooling is the hardest job they have ever done in their lives, and they are begging for the schools to open as well.

Unfortunately, summer is just around the corner, and for the first time ever, nobody is happy about it!

THREE MORE MONTHS AT HOME! YAY!

Mom is tired of watching Dad doing nothing during the quarantine, so she asked him to renovate our kitchen, and let me tell you, Dad is not happy!

He planned on fishing every day, but Mom messed up his plans in a BIG way.

😂

We can't hire anyone to do it because of the pandemic and quarantine, so Dad has to do everything alone.

Now we live in total disarray while Dad is changing the entire layout of the kitchen, installing new cabinets and countertops.

He may know how to do carpentry work, but trust me, he has no clue about plumbing and electricity.

I only hope he knows what he is doing because I wouldn't want the house to explode just because I felt like eating a burrito one day.

😁

JUNE

SATURDAY

The school year is finally over, which means we graduated to the next grade!

I can't believe I will be in sixth grade and start middle school in the fall!

MIDDLE SCHOOL, HERE I COME!

This time, I won't ask, "What could possibly go wrong?"!

I hope the pandemic will be over by then!

TUESDAY

Today, Dad suggested something completely insane.

Our whole family was sitting at the kitchen table, discussing our summer plans, when Dad said we should buy a trailer, like a two-bedroom towable RV, because traveling in a camper is safer during the pandemic than going to hotels and being around strangers.

Although many parks, resorts, and vacation spots were closed for three months during the quarantine, many hotels have opened up now, and some people are traveling again.

Mom and Dad received their first bookings for the rental homes as well, which is why Dad can take a loan to purchase the trailer.

Mom was very excited about the idea of owning a camper and said we could see so many interesting places.

Our island chain is connected to the mainland with bridges, so traveling in RVs is very popular around here, and many of our neighbors have luxurious trailers parked in their driveways.

But I was skeptical about this idea.

"Wait! What?" I said. "I don't want to be squeezed with everybody in the trailer! Let's find a remote RESORT!"

I am happy to go on a vacation—ANYTHING OUT OF THE HOUSE IS FINE WITH ME—but being stuck with my family in a trailer isn't better than being stuck in a five-bedroom home with a one-acre yard to run around.

But Dad said traveling in our own RV is exactly what we should do during the CORONAVIRUS OUTBREAK because we wouldn't need restaurants and hotels where we could catch the virus.

We wouldn't interact with any people because we would have everything we need inside the trailer.

He suggested taking the RV for a two-week vacation to some remote beach, away from the crowds, and enjoying the great outdoors.

We will cook all our meals, sleep inside the camper, have bonfires on the beach, sunbathe, and swim all day long.

Unlike me, Mom and Natalia are excited about this idea.

I'm not exactly happy to be stuck with my family in tight quarters for any length of time.

I usually keep myself at a distance from everyone, close enough to know what's going on but far enough away to maintain my personal space.

Living in a trailer where I need to share my bedroom with my sister is definitely a push for me.

UNSURPRISINGLY, Natalia is thrilled with the trip idea because now the family will be close together, and she won't sleep alone.

If it were up to her, she wouldn't separate from our parents for a minute. In fact, she would be perfectly fine in a kangaroo's pouch if Mom had one.

This, of course, doesn't surprise me.

Natalia and I have always been opposites.

I can't even stand when someone breathes next to me because I have this feeling they are stealing my air.

So, I suspect this trip will be a total disaster for me because there isn't much space to run away from anyone in a trailer on the road.

☹

Then Dad said we couldn't be in the trailer while on the road because the slide-outs of the trailer wouldn't be extended, so we would all sit with Dad in the truck.

That just ruined it for me completely because I don't know how to survive being strapped with a belt in one place for hours.

I just can't imagine it!

SATURDAY

I was sure this ridiculous idea of traveling in an RV would blow over, and Mom and Dad would soon cancel all the plans.

But today, Dad pulled up with a giant fifth-wheel trailer in front of the house.

When we stepped inside, this thing had two bedrooms, one and a half baths, a living room, and a kitchen.

It smelled wonderful because it was brand new. I have to admit, I was pretty impressed.

It looked cozy, and I could see how some families could live in it.

Our bedroom had its own powder room and two bunk beds on opposite sides.

Cabinets for clothes and a TV were under Natalia's bed. Under my bed was a sofa facing the TV. Basically, a bedroom with a living room setup.

Mom and Dad's bedroom was on the opposite side of the trailer.

Between the bedrooms were the living room, the kitchen, and the main bathroom with a shower.

Natalia ran back and forth, screaming with excitement, and Mom kissed Dad on the cheek (gross!).

The whole family seems happy with the vacation plans, but I remain skeptical.

😐

Mom often says I should always think positively about everything, but she doesn't understand how difficult that is for me.

Positivity is just not my thing!

☹

WEDNESDAY

This morning, Mom started researching oceanfront campgrounds outside of the islands.

Mom says it's not safe to travel to faraway places during the pandemic, and she wants to be a one-day driving distance away from our house in case one of us gets sick.

When spring turned into summer, cases with infected people started rising like dough on a pizza!

Numbers quadrupled everywhere because people were dying to go somewhere (literally and figuratively!).

😟

Because people's traveling increased the spread of the virus, Mom says we will be safe if we find that remote beach Dad was talking about.

This afternoon, Mom showed us a brochure with pictures of an oceanfront camping site, and I already *imagined myself swaying in a hammock in the shade of palm trees somewhere on a pristine beach, looking at turquoise waters and searching for dolphins. Alone and far away from tourists.*

It would take us a day of driving to get there, but I was willing to make the sacrifice.

I was kind of happy it was up to Mom to decide where we would go because if we left it up to Dad, we could end up in some questionable places.

Dad is not very good with instructions and directions, and he's gotten us lost so many times that nobody in the family trusts his judgment anymore.

Today, we began packing for the big trip.

Dad arranged to have someone take care of our lawn and pool. Mom asked the neighbor to water our houseplants while we are gone.

Mom ordered plenty of food to be delivered to our house so we could load the RV.

Natalia and I had a hard time deciding what to take on this two-week vacation, but Mom said we could take whatever we wanted because we had plenty of space in the trailer.

"Cool," I said, and I packed ten books, sketchbooks, paints, markers, a few canvases, and this diary.

Mom quickly regretted her answer when she saw Natalia packing all her dolls and stuffed animals.

"We don't have that much space!" she said. "Let me clarify, you both have two cabinets for your personal stuff, plus a closet for your clothes. You can take more than you would ever take if we were flying on a plane or driving by car, but there are limits."

Natalia didn't like giving up some of her toys, and for hours I watched her agonizing over what toys she should take and which ones she should leave behind, "hurting their feelings."

I came to the conclusion that traveling is much easier when you are a person of few needs like me.

☺

JULY

MONDAY

Today, we went on the road!

The cool thing about a trailer is we literally have everything with us.

All our clothes are in the cabinets, I have my favorite books, and Natalia has some of her toys.

The fridge and pantry are full of food, and we have plenty of water to last us two weeks.

Dad has enough gas for the entire road trip, so we don't need to stop anywhere on the way.

While on the road, we sat with Dad in his truck, with the trailer behind us.

After a day of driving, we finally pulled into the RV park.

Yes, there was a beach, palm trees, even a playground for kids—but boy, nothing was remote about that place!

Tons of RVs were parked one next to another, so close to each other—one RV's awning touched the slides of another.

People were everywhere—some wore masks, some did NOT, and kids swarmed the playground.

😮

Mom stared at the scene in horror. She said there was no way we could stay there because there were just too many people around.

"You're right," Dad said. "It wouldn't be safe to vacation around everyone during the pandemic."

Mom nodded, but I know she didn't care about the virus as much as the fact that she would have to be around so many strangers.

To her, staying in such proximity to other RVs is a nightmare. Pandemic or not, Mom likes her privacy and peace.

"Let's go somewhere into a forest, somewhere secluded where we can be by ourselves," Dad suggested.

Natalia was upset we had to leave because, for her, this was OBVIOUSLY a dream vacation—tons of kids screaming everywhere.

Dad started reversing out of our parking spot, but backing up a truck with a huge trailer was easier said than done.

He had a hard time turning the trailer and avoiding hitting something.

Back and forth, he tried and tried, and it seemed like we were stuck there.

Then we all had to get out to guide him. We put on our masks and started directing him, but he couldn't see us in his mirrors. The trailer was too long.

Finally, he got out of the spot, but unfortunately, he took out a traffic sign with him.

😮

He stepped outside to investigate the damage, and sure enough, the side of the trailer had a deep dent.

Dad was furious. He paced back and forth, his brows furrowed, his mouth tightly closed.

Then a man came over and said we would need to pay for the sign replacement, and I think Dad lost it because he kicked a nearby trash can with anger.

In the end, he took out his checkbook and paid for the sign AND the trash can.

When we were on the road again, Mom looked for remote forests where we could camp and be away from people.

The map showed many options, so she soon found a new destination.

As soon as we found a remote spot somewhere in the forest, Dad parked the trailer, and we all got out.

I wasn't sure what we were supposed to do there for two weeks, but Dad said it was a perfect opportunity for the whole family to do some old-fashioned camping.

He set up a foldable table and chairs and prepared a campfire.

Mom cooked dinner in the trailer, and we ate outside, surrounded by the warmth of a fire . . . and swarming bugs.

EXCITING!

Before bed, I decided to text Tracy.

> I'm stuck in a tight trailer with my whole family in the middle of nowhere!

 I'm stuck with my obnoxious brother and an annoying babysitter because my parents need to work and can't afford to take me on vacation!

Tracy has a brother who already goes to high school. His name is Danny, and he can be a true pain sometimes. He always makes fun of Tracy, which drives her crazy.

> You win. You have it worse.

 I always do.

Tracy always knows how to make me feel better.

TUESDAY

The first night in the camper was kind of scary because we could hear animals around our trailer and the sounds of owls in the distance.

It was strange to have my sister sleeping in the same room, but with the animal noises outside, I was glad I wasn't alone.

Today, we went on a hiking trail, but we soon returned when the bugs swarmed around us.

Besides, we were soaked from the mid-summer heat anyway.

🥵

Later, Natalia got a tick on her neck and screamed until Dad removed it inside the trailer.

After that, neither Natalia nor I wanted to go outside, so we sat in our room, enjoying the air conditioning.

🙂

Mom planned to enjoy relaxing on a beach chair outside of the trailer, but as soon as she found a comfortable spot, fire ants attacked her legs.

After that, her legs had nasty swollen red spots with blisters, and she was afraid to go outside as well.

Dad said he didn't want to sit inside the trailer, so he sat near the fire by himself.

Natalia and I chased each other inside, but Mom yelled that the whole trailer was shaking, so we took out our electronics and played games.

Unfortunately, we don't have internet here, so we are limited to some boring games that came with our tablets.

Before bedtime, Dad complained it wasn't real camping if we stayed inside all the time.

So, tomorrow, we will attempt to hike again, only this time we will be well prepared for the wild conditions around here.

WEDNESDAY

This morning, Mom and Dad prepared bacon and eggs for breakfast, and we decided to eat outside.

But while we were enjoying our meal, we heard some noises in the bushes nearby.

Dad got up and inspected the area around our camper, but he didn't find anything alarming.

However, as soon as he returned to the table, we heard something rustling nearby again.

Neither Mom nor Natalia nor I were interested in the potential encounter with a wild animal, so we brought our plates back to the trailer, where we peacefully ate at the dining room table in the air conditioning.

As you can imagine, Dad wasn't happy. We were just TOO COMFORTABLE!

"Being inside the trailer all the time is NOT real camping," he said.

I disagree with Dad. It's not like I can't see the forest through the window.

I mean . . . I know it's there.

😉

Dad asked us to prepare for another hiking trip, put on light clothing layers, wear hats, spray our arms and legs with bug spray, and bring plenty of water.

"We're going on an adventure," he said.

I really didn't see the point.

Why do we need to hike through the forest? The trees will look the same no matter where we go. But I said nothing and got ready for the excursion.

Each of us took a backpack to carry water, snacks, and bug spray.

Before we left, Mom asked Dad if he had something to protect us from the wild animals out there.

Well, that question sent Natalia into a panic attack, and she said she was too scared to go.

😬

Dad told her to calm down because he had a pocket knife with him.

"Are you planning to fight a bear with a three-inch pocket knife?" Mom asked.

"If we see a bear, we will move slowly away from him. I will grab a hiking stick to take with me if that makes you all feel better."

In fact, we all gathered hiking sticks after that conversation.

I don't know what we were thinking, but having something to swing in front of a wild animal made us all feel better for sure.

As I predicted, an hour into the woods, everything looked the same as the place we left behind.

The bug spray kept the mosquitos at bay, and we had plenty of water and snacks in our backpacks, so nobody was dehydrated.

It looked like this was going to be a successful hike when we suddenly heard a gunshot.

We immediately stopped in our tracks and looked around.

"What was that?" Mom asked.

"I don't see anything," Dad whispered.

Natalia started to cry, so I pulled her closer to me.

Then we heard another shot. And another. And another.

"We must be on hunting grounds! Run!" Dad screamed.

Hunting grounds? You mean . . . hunters shooting animals?

WHAT??

😲

I grabbed Natalia's hand, and we ran as quickly as we could, followed by our parents.

We heard gunshots all around us, and I wasn't sure what scared me more: the bullets or the animals they were hunting.

Mom was screaming, "PEOPLE ARE HERE!!"

But we didn't wait for the hunters to hear us.

We ran and ran and ran.

I had never been so scared for my life before!

When we reached our trailer, we locked the door and collapsed on the sofa.

Dad was mad and looked at Mom. "Did you choose this place from a list of registered campgrounds?"

Mom shook her head. "Not exactly ... We were looking for a REMOTE place ..."

"How remote did you want it to be? We must be close to hunting grounds! We won't be safe going into the woods anymore," Dad said.

I was just catching my breath after all that running when I said I would be fine with that.

"No," Dad said. "Tomorrow, we will go hiking in the opposite direction, and this time I will bring cooking

85

pots and will be banging them to make noise ALL THE WAY!"

Great! That sounds like a fun day! Ugh...

THURSDAY

As he promised, Dad brought two saucepans with him on today's hiking trip.

Like yesterday, we had everything we needed with us, but this time, the silence of the forest was ruined by Dad's banging pots.

And what's worse, he kept making STRANGE animal noises the entire time we walked.

I'm not sure who he was trying to scare away, the hunters or the animals, but TRUST ME, it WORKED!

PROBABLY EVERYONE IN THE AREA KNEW WE WERE IN THAT FOREST!

I bet he was heard in outer space!

😁

After this ear-piercing and headache-inducing hike, we were pleasantly surprised to stumble upon a lake.

Out of nowhere, there it was—a vast body of water stretching before our eyes for miles.

It was spectacularly beautiful, and yet . . . so desolate.

"Where are the resorts? Where are the houses? Why aren't there any people?" I asked.

"I don't know, but I'll tell you what, I LOVE IT!" Mom said and started removing her shoes.

"What are you doing?" Dad asked.

"What does it look like I'm doing? Swimming!" she said and ran into the water with her shorts and a tank top on.

"Cool! Swimming in our clothes! Best day ever!" Natalia said, removing her shoes and charging after Mom.

Dad and I looked at each other, then followed suit.

We laughed and splashed one another like crazy, and I really believed this was the beginning of a fun vacation.

Until I saw something staring at me on the bank of the lake.

"Alligators!!" I screamed and pointed to six gators basking in the sun, looking straight at us.

My heartbeat accelerated, and I started having difficulty breathing.

No wonder the lake was desolate.

I could see the panic in Mom's eyes, and Natalia started crying hysterically.

I turned toward Dad and said, "Maybe you should have brought the pots with you...."

"Shhh..." Dad said. "Let's slowly come out of the water.... Don't make any noises. Slowly... follow me."

We quietly walked behind Dad, who didn't take his eyes off the predators.

As soon as we reached the beach, we slowly picked up our sticks, pots, and shoes.

Dad pointed to the trail we came from. "You run as fast as you can in a straight line. Alligators are only quick for short distances."

As soon as he said it, all of us took off.

Just like yesterday, we ran for our lives.

But, of course, as we ran, Mom thought it was a GREAT idea to have a lesson.

With a shaking voice, Mom kept talking, "Alligators are reptiles and cold-blooded animals...." (Gasping for air.) "They sunbathe to keep their bodies warm so they can move." (Trying to catch her breath.) "Alligators existed before dinosaurs...." (Out of breath.) "The baby alligator's sex is determined by the temperature around the eggs, warmer for males and cooler for females...." (About to faint.)

"MOM!!" Natalia and I screamed. "STOP!"

ARE YOU KIDDING ME?

Does Mom really think this is a PERFECT opportunity to do homeschooling while we are trying NOT TO BE EATEN by the subject of discussion?

When Mom stopped giving us a lecture, we picked up speed.

When we reached our RV, we could hardly breathe.

"Why do we keep fighting for our lives?" Mom asked Dad. "That's not what a vacation should look like."

Dad nodded. "I give up. From now on, we stay put here until it's time to go. Everyone can do whatever they want."

Finally, we can relax!

SUNDAY

After a few days with my family trapped in a trailer, I'm ready to go home!

I don't like living in the camper because it is very tight for the four of us.

Anytime I need to go from one end to another, someone is always in my way, and I need to ask them to move.

You can't go anywhere without saying, "Excuse me," like five times.

The bathrooms are so tight that when I sit on the toilet, I can rest my head against the wall in front of me and doze off.

And the toilets always smell! No matter what treatments Dad puts inside the toilets, we live surrounded by the stench of human waste!

But the worst of it is that the walls are so thin that you can literally **HEAR EVERYTHING!**

I don't know about you, but I can't use a restroom if someone can hear me.

NOT A CHANCE!

This used to be a problem for me when I attended elementary school because the restroom was INSIDE the classroom, and you could hear every single noise kids were making in there!

I ended up at the nurse's station every other day having stomachaches because I couldn't use the bathroom with all those kids right behind the door, sitting in complete silence.

And just like at school, now I'm suffering from stomach issues again!

So, this afternoon, I told my whole family to leave the trailer so I could finally go to the bathroom.

But that's not the only problem!

The water pressure is so bad that nobody is allowed to use the kitchen sink when someone is in the shower!

If you use the sink in the kitchen, whoever is taking a shower loses water completely and screams.

The kitchen has practically no counter, so when Mom is cooking, she puts many things on the floor, and I always end up stepping into some kind of food!

Not having a dishwasher turned out to be a disaster because nobody seems to know how to wash dishes properly, and we eat our dinners on plates that have something hard stuck to them from the previous meal.

But, if that wasn't enough, today, tiny ants infested our trailer, and they got into all the dry food Mom had in the pantry.

EXTRA PROTEIN! SWEET!

But the worst part is—I can't ever be alone!

Not only are Mom and Dad always a few feet away, but also my sister never leaves my sight!

She wants to do everything with me and asks thousands of questions!

"What are you doing?"

"What are you reading?"

"What are you listening to?"

"What do you want to do next?"

"Where are you going?"

"Can I go with you?"

I'M GOING CRAZY!!

This is a violation of my personal space!!

WEDNESDAY

The camping vacation went from bad to worse.

Two days ago, we couldn't sleep because we heard a noise of an animal biting something INSIDE our trailer.

Yesterday morning, Dad inspected the trailer but couldn't find anything.

Natalia and I searched for any signs of an animal getting into the camper, as none of us would be able to sleep now, but we found no trace of the intruder.

Last night, we couldn't sleep again because the animal chewing noises lasted for hours.

This morning, Mom ran from the trailer, screaming because she woke up to a frog in her bed.

Later, Dad finally found the source of the noise that had kept us awake for the last two nights.

Rats—RATS!—were chewing the wood underneath our trailer and got inside the pantry as well.

Dad showed us the hole chewed up in the thin wall behind all the cans where we saw many rat droppings.

Mom had enough of our camping trip and told everyone we were going home.

She said she would NEVER vacation in the trailer again and made Dad sell it in the RV trading place on the way home.

She ordered a limousine, where we stuffed all our things, and a chauffeur took us home.

"I guess we're not gonna travel to those interesting places you talked about, right?" I asked, enjoying the spacious leather seats and sipping on a fruity drink from the minibar inside the limo.

"Not in a trailer, that's for sure," Mom said.

I nodded. If we ever travel to faraway places, I hope it will be in style like this!

So far, the ride in that fancy limousine with our own chauffeur is my favorite part of the camping trip with my family this summer!

AUGUST

MONDAY

Things are slowly getting better with the pandemic. Stores stocked up on food, department stores and restaurants opened, and people are moving on with their daily lives.

However, many events and festivals are still canceled, and you need to socially distance yourself from other people—six feet apart—and wear a mask to prevent the virus from spreading.

In some places, we can enjoy the outdoors without the masks as long as we are away from others.

Mom and Dad believe in social distancing from other people because we don't want to bring the virus to Grandma.

All the elderly are at higher risk of dying from the virus, and since millions of people have died from the coronavirus worldwide, Mom says no meetings with people are worth the risk.

The only sad part about stores stocking up on products is that Natalia and I lost our toilet paper-making business and had to announce bankruptcy.

Although people paid mostly with small coins, it was still a good thing going during these apocalyptic times.

Mom says it's a great economy lesson in the real world.

She said when the stores were out of toilet paper, and we were offering our rolls of drawings for tips—we had MONOPOLY and a great DEMAND, which resulted in better PROFIT.

But when the stores started selling toilet paper again, that created COMPETITION, so we lost DEMAND because toilet paper is now widely available, which resulted in LOSS of profit.

Mom says that competition keeps prices low and affordable.

I don't know why this is a good thing since you can make more money when you have a monopoly.

But I guess if I'm the one BUYING stuff, I would prefer lower prices and more places to shop.

So, although we lost our tips, Mom is happy people stopped congregating by our gate, which was really stressing her out.

As you can see, sometimes parents have little appreciation for child labor.

FRIDAY

Today, Dad decided to take Natalia, Mom, and me on a fishing trip around the islands.

He said he's had enough of staying home and waiting for the pandemic to end.

Because we have a waterfront property, our boat is docked at the pier in front of our house.

Before the pandemic, we used to go on the boat a lot. But during the quarantine, boats were not allowed to congregate on the sandbars, and all restaurants with docks were closed.

And since Mom asked Dad to renovate the kitchen, he hasn't been fishing for months.

Because Dad finished installing our brand-new kitchen and Mom is happy, he is ready to venture into the vast ocean again.

My sister loves fishing, so she was excited about the family day on the water.

Mom packed our lunch, and soon we were cruising on our way to get our next great catch.

After a peaceful ride, Dad stopped the boat in front of a massive bridge, which used to be a railroad in the past.

"Big fish like to congregate near bridges because the strong currents near the bridges bring smaller prey they feed on," Dad said.

Unlike Natalia, I don't like touching the slimy squid, so Dad hooked the bait for me.

Mom was reading a book while the three of us stood with our rods set, waiting.

Unsurprisingly, Natalia was the first one to catch a fish. And it wasn't just any fish!

It was a mangrove snapper!

She was so excited!

She removed the hook from its mouth all by herself and was just about to throw it back into the water when Dad screamed, "NO! It's a delicious fish for dinner!"

Natalia narrowed her eyes. "I'm not eating my catch."

Dad took the fish from her hands. "Baby, this is fine dining here. And with the empty stores that we witnessed during the quarantine, I think we shouldn't be wasteful of such a great dinner."

"Fine, you can eat this one. But I hope I won't catch any edible fish ever again!" Natalia said and cast her line.

Shortly after that, I felt a tug on my rod.

"Bring it in!" Dad said.

I started to reel it in, and Dad got ready with the net.

And you will not believe what I caught!

A small hammerhead shark!

"I caught a shark!" I screamed. "I can't believe I caught a shark!"

Dad caught it with a net and brought it on the boat.

The shark was flipping and flopping, fighting for its life.

"Quickly, let it go!" Natalia screamed.

Dad took out the hook, we took a photo with the shark, and I let it go.

The shark swam away in a hurry.

"Do you know that sharks have no bones?" Mom said, always teaching us something—even in the summer! "They have a soft cartilage, just like our ears and noses do."

"Why don't they have bones?"

"Cartilage helps them bend, twist, and turn."

"Which means, without bones, they can be better predators," I said.

"Exactly."

Next, Dad caught a large barracuda!

That fish scared me because it had many sharp teeth, and Dad had to fight to remove the hook from its mouth.

Because they are not edible, I was happy to see the barracuda go!

When I thought we were finally done with fishing, Dad had another tug on his line.

But this time, the line went crazy!

"A tarpon!" Dad screamed. "My dream fish! Get ready for a fight, girls!"

Mom quickly got up and started the engine.

She said she would need to chase the fish while Dad was trying to bring it to the boat.

"They are very aggressive, excellent fighters!" he said. "Great trophy fish but not edible."

"Thank goodness," Natalia said. She hates killing fish.

Soon, we were chasing after the tarpon.

I could see its silver back shining in and out of the water.

All I could hear was the line hissing on Dad's bent rod.

"It will break your fishing rod," Mom said.

"No, it won't. I'll get the monster."

And sure enough, after an hour of a fight, Dad brought the tarpon on the boat.

We quickly took a photo of Dad with his great catch.

Dad removed the hook from its mouth and started to put the fish in the water when suddenly a huge shark came to our boat with its mouth wide open.

"AAAAAAA!!" we all screamed!

As soon as Dad threw the tarpon back into the water, the massive shark attacked the tarpon, shredding it into pieces right before our eyes!

I'M TRAUMATIZED FOR LIFE!!

My heart was pounding, my hands were shaking, and I thought we would die!

"You never told me such huge sharks swim where WE SWIM!!" I said to Dad.

He said that sharks love to congregate around bridges and strong currents because that's where they have plenty of smaller fish to catch.

Especially during tarpon season, waters near bridges are full of large sharks feasting on their prey.

"It's safe to swim near the beach because sharks are not interested in humans, but you wouldn't catch me swimming near the bridges," he said.

I screamed,

"I'M NEVER GETTING INTO THE OCEAN OR ANY DESOLATE LAKE EVER AGAIN!!"

"Honey, shark attacks are very rare. They really are not interested in humans. You will be fine swimming in the ocean."

"Don't count on it!" I said. And I meant it!

WEDNESDAY

Mom and Dad have been trying to persuade me to go to the beach with them for the past few days, but I refused.

I don't want to be near the ocean. I'm not swimming around the sharks, that's for sure!

Today, Mom said that the best way to conquer my fears is to face them, so my parents took me back on the boat to snorkel on the local coral reef.

I was reluctant to go, but Dad promised he would be with me at all times.

Although it is still SUMMER, Mom gave us a lesson about how coral reefs are made.

"Corals are made of tiny creatures called polyps, which live in a colony on skeletons of other hard coral polyps. When they die, new corals live on their skeletons, building layer after layer of a skeleton, and over thousands . . . even a million years—the reef grows. The colorful tree-like or flower-like corals are soft, and they decorate the reef."

Natalia and I listened to Mom's lesson on the way to the reef. By now, we are used to Mom teaching us on the go, no matter where we are.

POLYP

When we tied the boat to the floating buoy at the reef, many other boaters were already there, snorkeling around.

I felt better to see other people in the water, so I put on my wet suit, snorkel, and fins and jumped into the water after Mom, Dad, and Natalia.

As soon as I opened my eyes, I regretted my decision. I saw round pink jellyfish floating around.

I immediately swam up to the ladder, climbed into the back of the boat, and sat down on the deck.

"What happened?" Mom asked when she approached the boat, holding on to the ladder.

"Did you see how many jellyfish are there?"

"Sylvia, it's a season for jellyfish right now, but this is why we made you put on a wet suit. Besides, jellyfish have no brain, so they won't follow you. Just stay away from them, and you will be fine."

"Jellyfish may not have a brain, but I do! And my brain tells me not to go into that water."

I can't imagine what it would be like to have no brain and only go wherever the ocean currents take me.

Although I was uncomfortable swimming around the jellyfish, I saw Natalia happily swimming with Dad, so I knew I had to tough this one out.

When I joined Dad and Natalia, I found myself among other swimmers, which made me feel safer.

I figured if I stayed in the middle of the group, I would be safe from any predators.

And that's when I saw the shark. It wasn't as big as the one that devoured the tarpon, but still.

My heart started pounding like crazy, and I emerged from the water, trying to take a breath of fresh air.

Dad floated near me. "The shark won't hurt you. It is on the bottom and is only interested in small fish. People snorkel here every day."

He grabbed my hand, and we swam together.

Dad was right—the shark paid no mind to us. It was peacefully circling the bottom of the reef.

A large barracuda with sharp teeth passed near us, and Dad squeezed my hand to let me know I was safe.

I don't know how safe I was—jellyfish, barracudas, a shark—but I took my mom's advice and FACED MY FEARS.

I swam around with the rest of the snorkelers, enjoying the colorful world of the reef.

Suddenly, a school of yellowtail snappers surrounded me. It was amazing! They were not scared of me at all.

I twirled around, letting them pass me in all directions.

Then, even more of them came, and I couldn't see anything at this point—just one mass of yellow fish.

That's when I realized the school of fish would be a great buffet for a larger fish, like a shark, so I quickly freed myself from the snappers.

As I emerged from the school of fish, I bumped into something.

With a pounding heart, I turned around to see an ENORMOUS goliath grouper!

Although I thought I would die of fear, the grouper looked as if I had just disturbed its sleep. The creature had no interest in me at all!

As soon as the other snorkelers saw the massive fish, everyone swam around it, taking its photos with underwater cameras.

Since I was the closest to it, I ended up in their pictures, and I felt like a celebrity.

I even started posing for them so they could catch me from the right angle. I imagined what it would be like to be famous. . . .

As underwater flashes went off, I gave a bow, and everyone attempted to clap.

That took away all the anxiety I had about being around all those creatures, and I enjoyed snorkeling with my family for the rest of the day.

My family was right; if we all respect each other, animals and people can coexist in this beautiful underwater world.

You just never know when a day can turn out to be an awesome adventure!

SATURDAY

I love my sister and all, but after months of quarantine with only Natalia, I'm ready to meet with some people my age.

This morning, I asked Mom if I could invite Tracy, Alex, and Grace to our place to hang out in our pool.

But she said she couldn't allow other kids to come during the pandemic because their parents work in public places and might bring the virus home, after which our friends can transfer it to us.

She suggested visiting Grandma, who lives on a different island, instead.

Well, that was all I needed to hear because I love visiting Grandma!

Today, when we visited Grandma, we baked cookies and cakes, watched a movie, and fed the chickens together.

She showed us how to do gardening and sewing.

She is all about teaching us home economics, so when we become wives, we'll know how to do everything.

But that's just crazy talk for me because I'm not planning to get married at all.

Instead, I plan to have lots of money to travel all over the world and hire people to do domestic tasks for me.

So, sometimes I think I'm wasting my time learning how to do all those things, but with the pandemic going on, there's nothing better to do anyway.

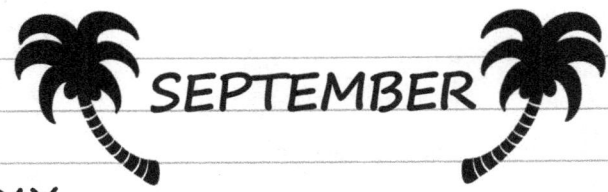

SEPTEMBER

<u>MONDAY</u>
I CAN'T BELIEVE I'M IN SIXTH GRADE AND STARTED MIDDLE SCHOOL TODAY!!

This year, most kids started doing virtual classes where they see their teachers online, listen to the lectures, and do tons of work at home.

Some schools alternate days between in-person and virtual learning. This way, only half of the kids are at school on any day while the other half stay home and attend online. Then they switch.

Because our islands are small and don't have enough hospital beds for everyone, our schools remain closed and offer online classes to prevent the virus from spreading.

When I heard about this school year's arrangements on TV, I was so happy to be homeschooled by my mom.

I know it's only till the pandemic is over, but I will get any weeks without homework I can get!

But my excitement didn't last long.

Today, when I saw my sixth-grade curriculum books, I thought I would have a heart attack.

Packages on top of packages were delivered to our doorstep.

You may wonder what middle school looks like at home, and you may even think it can't be all that scary.

It is. When your mom is a teacher, you can't get away with anything. She makes sure you WILL know the information.

TRUST ME!

You know how . . . kids live double lives—misbehaving at school but playing cool at home to get bonus stuff from their parents?

You know how . . . many parents believe their kids are "perfect," and it is absolutely not possible their child does all those awful things at school?

You know what I'm talking about.

Yeah, none of that is possible at home.

Your mom knows every detail of your student life, your progress or lack of it, so there is no chance to pretend to be her perfect child.

This means, usually, you are DOOMED.

☹

To get anything from your parents, you actually need to show progress in your studies!

Are you still jealous? I don't think so.

In the spring, we read science and social studies books TOGETHER. We practiced math TOGETHER, and Mom cut me some slack in memorizing all the formulas.

But now that I am in sixth grade, Mom says things are serious, and I need to memorize lots of facts, names, formulas, and rules.

While she is teaching us at home, Mom wants to cover ancient civilizations.

I'm supposed to memorize what is inside cells and the entire human body!

And the MATH!

Negative numbers! What in the world are negative numbers?

Sometimes, I think adults don't have anything better to do than make kids' lives miserable.

If I were a teacher, I would focus on only ART so all kids can make this world a beautiful place to live.

But Mom says, to hang art, you need walls, and no buildings can be constructed without knowing math and science.

Mom always has an answer to everything, so sometimes I am tired of fighting my arguments, and I do what she asks me.

Sometimes.

Instead of being a follower most of my life, I would like to be a LEADER one day, like my sister is among her peers.

Kids always want to be like Natalia, and everybody wants to be her friend.

Since she was little, kids wanted to wear clothes similar to Natalia's, pigtails as she does, and buy toys identical to hers. (I'm rolling my eyes here.)

Then again, maybe being a leader wouldn't be such a great thing.

Come to think of it, nobody likes to be copied, and I probably would be frustrated to see everyone look like ME and behave like ME.

Mom often says that trying to fit in only takes away a part of who you are.

And I think there is some truth in it.

Maybe being DIFFERENT from everyone else is better than trying to be THE SAME.

Mom never tries to fit in with everyone.

She does what she wants, when she wants, and how she wants it.

And, to my surprise, she gets lots of respect from people for that.

This is why many people call Mom and ask her about homeschooling now that sending kids to school during the CORONAVIRUS outbreak practically risks your life.

I'm happy I'm writing this diary then.

Maybe one day someone will read this diary and, for once, they will know what it is like to be ME!

WEDNESDAY

Natalia and I love staying home all day, playing games on our tablets after lessons are over.

Mom always complains we spend too much time glued to electronics, but we hardly ever listen.

It's not surprising then that Mom isn't happy that we have to be quarantined at home because of the pandemic.

Now we have a perfect excuse not to go outside.

We're practically forced to stay home and play on our tablets.

Normally, Mom wants me to interact with real children instead of playing games.

I tell her I do play with other kids—just online.

We invite each other into our online platforms to create things together on the screen.

Mom says it's not the same as hanging out with children outside.

Honestly, I cannot imagine how the real world could be more interesting than the one I created myself!

☺

Today's history lesson was about the first humans on Earth: the homo habilis, the homo erectus, and the modern humans—the homo sapiens—and we learned how they mastered the use of stones for tools and fire for cooking.

After watching that movie with Dad about the man whose plane crashed, and he landed on a desert island for years without civilization, I was really paying attention to Mom's lesson.

During these apocalyptic times, you just never know when you may need to resolve to primitive ways of life.

When we finished our lessons, we continued to play online games.

After a while, Mom had enough of us sitting inside the house, playing games on our tablets all day long, so she told us to go outside.

"We don't want to go anywhere. Nobody's around!" I said, staring at the screen.

"You can't spend all your childhood playing computer games! When I was your age, we always played outside," she said.

I sighed, not taking my eyes off the game. "But this is the twenty-first century, Mom. Kids don't do that anymore."

"Well, I don't care what other kids do! Under my watch, you won't be on electronics for more than an hour a day!"

"Mom, we'll get Corona if we go out there!" I said in a serious voice.

"No, you won't. I don't want you to leave the gate. I just want you to play outside on our property."

"Do we have to?" Natalia asked.

"It's too hot, Mom," I added.

Mom narrowed her eyes and pointed to the front door. "Go outside, get dirty, get in trouble, for goodness' sake!"

Within a minute, Mom kicked us out of the house.

I wasn't pleased to be forced outside like that, but Natalia had this smile spread across her face, and I knew she was on to something.

"Mom told us we could get in trouble," she said, "so we can do whatever we want."

"True..."

She did have a point.

This could be an opportunity of a lifetime.

😉

Natalia and I looked at each other, and we both knew if getting in trouble was mentioned, we would need to venture into the big world behind the gate.

We left our property unnoticed, and when we were strolling down the street, we saw THE DUDE painting the front door of his house.

Like I said before, THE DUDE is the teenager who works in our local supermarket and catches my sister and me riding on the shopping carts.

I guess his mom had enough of him watching TV all day long during the pandemic and sent him to work.

He must have been just about done because he started putting the roller and paint away when he noticed us.

He spit on the ground like he always does.

"GROSS!" I yelled.

"You're gross!" he responded and went inside his house.

What a jerk!

We continued on our walk. It rained last night, so the streets were wet. We jumped into every puddle we saw.

Then we got this idea to slide on the mud on the nearby hiking trail.

This spot always floods during rains, and today wasn't any different.

The water had receded, leaving behind a long stretch of soft mud.

First, we stepped far enough away to have plenty of space to gain speed, running.

Then off we ran to slide on the mud.

Sometimes we kept our balance, but most of the time, we landed on the ground.

We had an awesome time, but our clothes were ruined, and we were completely covered in mud.

On our way back, my sister grabbed my hand and smiled. "THE DUDE is gone."

"Do you want to fix his boots?" I asked Natalia.

She nodded and smiled mischievously.

As you can see, younger siblings can have a bad influence on you very quickly.

I concocted this idea to leave muddied prints of our bodies on his freshly painted white front door.

Natalia giggled.

We quietly approached his house and pressed ourselves against his front door.

When we pulled away, two muddied figures remained. We gave each other a thumbs up and started running home.

☺

But before we reached our house, we spotted Mom on the street, calling our names. "Sylvia! Natalia! Where are you?"

"We are here!" I screamed and waved my hand. "Over here!"

Mom looked at us, but I could tell she wasn't sure whether those two muddy figures were truly her daughters.

"I was so worried! Where were you? What happened to you?" she asked as soon as we approached her.

Natalia jumped with joy. "We had so much fun playing in the mud, Mommy!"

"Girls, I thought you were lost. I've been looking for you. You were gone for two hours!"

"Only two hours?" I asked. "You told us to go outside and have fun."

"I don't want you to do that anymore," she said.

"You don't want us to be outside?" I couldn't believe my ears. The dream of playing online games all day long may finally come true for me!

"Of course not! I mean . . . yes! I just need to know where you are. I worry about you when you aren't home. This pandemic is making me crazy! I'm afraid you'll get sick!"

"Okay, we were just doing what you asked us," I said, knowing I'd proven my point: it's just safer to play on the tablet.

When we got home, we planned to take a shower, but someone knocked on the door.

When Mom went to the foyer to open the door, I had this nagging feeling something was up.

And sure enough, THE DUDE and his mother were standing outside!

With their face masks on, they told Mom we had destroyed their front door with mud, completely exaggerating this whole thing!

Mom was mad instantly and demanded we apologize and clean their door right away.

I couldn't believe she didn't even want to hear our side of the story!

I thought about denying it, but the mud all over our clothes was pretty solid evidence!

We had to follow THE DUDE to his house (six feet behind him) and scrub the door until it was clean.

While we worked hard over there, we saw THE DUDE peeking from his window, laughing.

In the end, we got in trouble for getting in trouble, which Mom told us to do in the first place.

And they wonder why a generation gap exists between parents and their kids.

MONDAY

This morning, Mom and Dad discussed some "important matters" behind their closed bedroom door. We were told to occupy ourselves during that time.

Although the thought of me having extra time on my tablet was exciting, neither one of us wanted to miss the opportunity to eavesdrop on some family secrets.

We tiptoed upstairs, where their bedroom is located and sat quietly near the door.

We couldn't hear everything they were saying, but we picked up a few pieces of their conversation.

Basically, Mom told Dad she worried whether they would be okay financially during these challenging times.

As I mentioned before, Mom and Dad own vacation houses they rent to people. Unfortunately, half of their guests canceled their reservations for this entire year because of the coronavirus outbreak and requested refunds of their deposits.

Although we have slowly started receiving bookings, Mom and Dad's income suffered drastically during the pandemic, which means by now, we are barely making it financially.

When Natalia heard that, she got upset, so I needed to move us back downstairs so she wouldn't give us away.

She said she worried that if our family ran out of money, we would have to sell our rental business and move out of the islands.

I know why she worried about it. During the pandemic, a lot of businesses were forced to close to prevent the virus from spreading, so many families couldn't afford to live in the tropics anymore and needed to move to places where housing was cheaper.

Although I understood her concerns, I told Natalia she was being too dramatic and that we would be fine.

I wasn't as worried as she was, so I plopped myself on the couch to catch up on BUILDING WORLDS on my tablet.

My sister, on the other hand, started packing her brand-new pink backpack with items I couldn't see.

"What are you doing?" I asked her.

"I'll earn money myself."

I burst out laughing because I thought she was joking.

"And how are you gonna do this?"

"By washing people's windows. I'll knock on people's doors. I have cleaning supplies in my backpack."

I still believed she was kidding, but when she put on her mask and headed out the door, I realized she was serious.

I tried to concentrate on my game, but I felt slightly guilty because I was lazy and wasn't working with Natalia.

I was getting pretty upset that she left me hanging like this. This whole situation made me uncomfortable.

Mom and Dad were trying to figure out our life upstairs while my sister worked hard to make ends meet somewhere in the neighborhood.

And all I cared about was winning this game.

I was battling between playing and going after Natalia, but my online friends joined the game, and I decided to stay.

But honestly, I don't know what I would have done if Natalia hadn't shown up at the door when she did. That was a close call!

I don't know how long she was gone, but when she barged inside the house, she was holding a five-dollar bill, grinning with excitement. "I earned money!"

I jumped off the couch and inspected it.

I couldn't believe my eyes as I stared at the crisp new bill. I was so jealous that I could hardly breathe.

Soon, our parents returned downstairs, and Natalia immediately told them about her earnings.

She said the next-door neighbor had let her wash the one window she could reach outside and paid her five dollars.

Mom and Dad looked shocked that she had left the house without them knowing and that Natalia would knock on strangers' doors. Especially during the pandemic!!

"Don't worry, I stayed six feet apart from the neighbor and only cleaned the window outside," Natalia said.

I was sure she would get in trouble for that, but instead, Mom and Dad congratulated her.

They kissed her and hugged her. They wanted to frame the dollar bill she earned in the real world!

Mom and Dad were so proud of Natalia that they called Grandma and some of their friends to tell them about her entrepreneurship.

Everyone wanted to speak to my sister and congratulate her.

Although I tried not to pay any attention to my sister's unexpected fame, I couldn't hide my frustration and jealousy.

I wanted that five-dollar bill and everyone's attention, too!

☹

But all good things come to an end, and Natalia's successful day soon turned into a nightmare.

In the evening, Mom wanted to wash her mirror in the bathroom and asked Natalia where she had put the cleaner.

My sister said all the cleaning supplies were in her pink backpack.

Mom looked for the backpack, but she couldn't find it anywhere.

Natalia ran around the house, searching, but nobody could find it.

"Honey, do you remember where you put it last?" Mom asked her.

It always frustrates me when Mom asks that question because if we could remember where we put our things, they wouldn't be lost!

"I left it in front of our gate because I was cleaning the house across the street!" She burst into tears.

Mom told her to calm down because it was only cleaning supplies, and she was sure the backpack still was where she had left it.

But Natalia couldn't stop crying, so we all left the house to look for her backpack.

We searched for it everywhere, but couldn't find it.

Mom spoke to the neighbor who had let Natalia wash her window, but she didn't see the backpack at all. "Natalia came with only a cleaner in her hand."

Mom thanked her for allowing Natalia to earn money and apologized for bothering her again.

Suddenly, Natalia became very pale, and I knew right away that not only the cleaning supplies but also something important was in that backpack, too.

Now I know why they say the blood drains from someone's face. It sure looks like it.

When we returned home, we got ready for bed.

Mom and Dad felt bad for Natalia because she had lost her favorite backpack while doing such an admirable thing.

They catered to her all evening, and I was having enough.

Then, just before bedtime, Mom barged into the living room and asked where my sister's money was. The jar was missing from Natalia's dresser.

We have been receiving a small allowance from Mom and Dad for helping them with the house chores.

At first, Natalia spent it all on toys, but since the pandemic started, we both saved it in our money jars.

My sister seemed lost for words, averting her eyes, so Mom already knew!

"Did you lose your money, Natalia?" she demanded.

My sister burst into tears. "Yes. I put the jar in my backpack!"

Mom put her hands on her face, clearly in shock. "Why would you do that? You had a few hundred dollars saved! Why would you take the money outside of the house?"

"I wanted the jar with me so I could put my earned money inside!" my sister said and started crying hysterically.

"You know, you shouldn't let her have her own money. She's too young," I said, browsing through a magazine.

"Obviously!" Mom said and sent Natalia to her room.

Before bedtime, Mom and Dad had a talk with my sister. They explained how sorry they felt for her, but she had been irresponsible, and this was a lesson.

Although I looked more responsible than my sister tonight, it was a bittersweet victory.

😔

I would be terribly upset if I lost all my money, so I decided to do something to cheer her up, and I came up with a plan to help our parents.

TUESDAY

This morning, Natalia woke up to a letter from me and twenty dollars inside the envelope.

She hugged me, smiling, and although I don't like hugs, it kind of felt good.

My parents were very proud of me for doing that, although I wasn't looking for praise this time.

In the afternoon, I called for a family meeting at the kitchen table.

When everyone was seated, I explained my plan to Mom and Dad. "Natalia and I are aware that our income during the pandemic is suffering, and we would like to help you."

Mom smiled. "Thank you, girls, but I can't allow you to go to strangers and wash their windows like Natalia did yesterday. It was an ambitious thing to do, but you both are too young to have side jobs like that."

I nodded. "Unfortunately, Natalia has lost her money, but I still have the savings I earned doing house chores. I also saved the tips we received from the 'sale' of the toilet paper we made from our drawings at the beginning of the pandemic. I would like you to have my savings," I said.

Dad smiled. "Honey, we really appreciate it, but we wouldn't take your money. If it gets to the point where we are really short, I will get a job as a carpenter."

"I have a plan, Dad," I said. "How about from this point on, Natalia and I help with the house chores WITHOUT the allowance? Would that help?"

Natalia nodded. "Yes! We want to help!"

Mom and Dad exchanged glances and smiled at each other.

"We are very proud of you, girls. You are certainly growing up," Mom said.

"Does this mean you won't sell our business and move out of the islands?" Natalia asked.

"Oh, girls, is that what you were thinking? No, we are here to stay. This is home now, no matter what happens," Mom answered and gave us a hug and a kiss.

Dad hugged us and told us that helping Mom around the house without expecting anything is a very grown-up thing to do.

I feel better now that I can help my parents, after all. But helping Mom and Dad is not the only thing on my mind.

I know I have to find out what happened to my sister's pink backpack and all her money! No matter what, I will find it!

WEDNESDAY

Today, I was determined to find out who stole my sister's backpack with all her money in it.

The time has come to put on a BIG SISTER hat and solve the mystery.

This whole time, I've been suspecting one person behind this stealing.

If you're thinking about THE DUDE, then we're thinking the same way.

I figure he probably wanted to have his payback time after our incident with the mud on his door.

Besides, he doesn't like us because we chase each other on the shopping carts.

This means—he has MOTIVE!

But every detective knows you need solid PROOF to send someone to jail—or in our case, condemn him in the neighborhood forever.

My plan of action was simple: I would ask him directly if he took the backpack and give him the opportunity to plead GUILTY.

☺

I had my cell phone with me to record his statement and have the proof I needed.

I put on my face mask and headed to his house.

After I knocked at his door, THE DUDE showed up at the entrance.

"What do you want?" he asked.

"The TRUTH," I said, narrowing my eyes.

"What?"

Obviously, he had no clue what I was asking him.

"My sister's backpack was stolen the other day. She left it right outside of our gate, and it was gone within an hour."

He yawned. "So?"

"We both know no other kids live on the street other than you and us. I don't think our elderly neighbors were interested in a kid's pink backpack."

"And you think I wanted a PINK backpack?" He laughed.

For a moment, I thought he got me. "It's the twenty-first century, DUDE."

He stopped laughing. "You must be out of your mind if you think I would want ANYBODY to see me with a pink backpack. Get lost!" He slammed the door.

But I didn't believe him!

I decided to set a trap for the thief to catch him in action and record it on my cell phone as EVIDENCE.

I put one of Natalia's pink beach bags outside of the gate, and I hid nearby in the bushes.

I waited for about forty minutes before my legs started to go numb, and I got hungry.

I sprinted into the house, grabbed a granola bar, and returned to my hiding spot.

I don't know how long I was gone—maybe twenty minutes—because I needed to use the bathroom.

When I returned to the gate, I couldn't believe my eyes.

THE BEACH BAG WAS GONE!

I was fuming inside!

How could this happen?

How am I gonna tell Natalia that her beach bag was gone, too?

But most of all, WHO was doing it?

I was disappointed I had missed the opportunity to catch the thief, and I promised myself it would NEVER happen again!

THURSDAY

Natalia is upset about losing her favorite beach bag (how was I supposed to know it was her favorite?), and Mom is mad that I even took it and left it behind the gate.

No one seems to understand it was a necessary sacrifice!

Today, I was just about to give up this whole search for the thief when I saw someone hanging around our gate.

I immediately ran outside, but when I got there, nobody was there.

That's it! I'd had enough.

I decided to ask all my neighbors if they saw anybody snooping around our property.

I took my face mask from my pocket and walked to the first house. Then another. And another.

I explained to everyone the mystery of the missing backpack and asked questions like, "Have you seen anyone hanging out near our gate lately? Do you know if there are any vacationers or visitors on our street?"

But everyone shook their heads, just as puzzled as I was.

But then, this one old lady said something that caught my attention. "You know, Sylvia, a new family moved onto our street a week ago, two houses away from mine. I saw a kid's bike in their driveway."

What? A new family? Another kid in our neighborhood? Hmm . . . That was the clue I needed!

I thanked her for this valuable information and headed toward the house she had pointed out.

Once and for all, the mystery would be solved NOW.

I marched up their stairs and rang the bell.

A boy about my age opened the door. He had dark hair and the face of a model from a kids' clothing magazine.

He eyed me with curiosity and smiled, showing perfectly straight white teeth.

Suddenly, I was very aware of the stain on my T-shirt, that I might not have brushed my hair today, that my flip-flops still had mud from the other day, and that my two front teeth overlapped a tiny bit.

My mask covered my teeth, but I couldn't do anything about my messy appearance.

The boy removed a mask from his pocket and put it on his face. "Can I help you?"

"Huh . . . ?" I said, forgetting for a moment why I had come here.

The backpack. The beach bag.

Somehow, I had my doubts that this stranger on our street had anything to do with missing GIRLY items.

GREAT! Now I was stuck. I had to say something, but what?

"Um . . . There have been . . . a series of stealing cases reported on our street recently . . . wondering . . . whether you may have seen anyone . . . suspicious hanging around our gate in the past few days?" I mumbled.

"The house with the gate is yours?"

"Yes," I said, wondering whether he knew something.

"I haven't seen anyone, but I don't really know anyone here yet."

I nodded, standing there and not knowing what to say. Where was my tongue when I needed it?

"I'm Jeremy." He extended his hand, then quickly put it in his pocket.

This stupid pandemic!! People can't be normal anymore!

I felt blood rushing to my cheeks, and I hoped he couldn't see my reddened face behind my mask. "I'm Sylvia."

"Well, it's nice to meet you. I've seen you around the street."

Oh no! I hope he didn't see me covered in that mud the other day! I would die if he had.

"If you see anything suspicious around my gate, could you let me know?" I asked.

"I'll keep my eyes open," he said and gave me a wink.

I nodded and turned around to leave.

But, when I was walking home, my heart was pounding, and I had this feeling it had something to do with the stranger on our street.

FRIDAY

Today, I needed to talk to Tracy about this new neighbor. I dialed her number and was happy to hear her voice.

"Hey, girl," she said.

"Hey, how are you?" I asked.

"Miserable! I miss hanging out with you."

"I know. This pandemic sucks!"

"Have you heard on the news that schools started opening up in more places?" Tracy asked.

"Yes. Do you think our school will open soon?"

"I hope so! My cousin's school opened recently and started in-person learning. She says it's a nightmare, though. Most of her classes are still online, but they let them go to school for certain classes. They only allow a few kids at a time. They have to sit apart from each other, and they have to wear those awful masks all the time! They eat their lunch separated, and they have to stay six feet apart during recess."

"Wow, it sounds morbid."

"It's a school of horror," Tracy said in a deep voice.

I laughed when I pictured some of the bullies from school having to go through that.

Imagine that! Not being able to touch a kid if you're a bully!

That made me think about Max Gunov, the bully from Natalia's class. He must be beside himself during the pandemic!

"So, how are you doing?" she asked.

I told her about the missing backpack and beach bag and how I was looking for the thief.

"That's crazy! Who would steal a kid's things on the street where only older folks live?"

I told her I suspected THE DUDE had done it, but I had no proof. And then I told her about the new boy on our street.

"What's his name?" Tracy asked.

"Jeremy."

"That's cool. You'll have another kid to hang out with nearby."

Right! Like I am such a people person and hanging out with kids I don't know is natural for me.

We talked for another half an hour before I ended the call.

After that, I tried to come up with a plan to catch the thief and make him pay for stealing my sister's things.

But I had a hard time focusing because my thoughts drifted to the new boy on our street.

Another call disturbed my daydreaming, this time from Alex.

Because I haven't seen him for months, I'm always happy to hear his voice.

"What are you doing?" he asked in his cheerful voice.

"Planning a trap to throw a bad guy into jail."

"Details, please!" he asked with excitement.

I told him all about the missing things and my suspicions about THE DUDE. But I never mentioned Jeremy.

"It sounds like THE DUDE definitely might have done it to play pranks on you girls," he said.

"He's the only one on the street who is out to get us."

"So, how are you gonna catch him in the act?"

"I don't know yet, but I'll come up with something for sure."

"Hey, Sylvia . . . ?"

I waited for him to finish, but all I heard was silence. "Yes?"

"When this is all done, and we can finally hang out together again, I'll take you to this new ice cream store in town. They have, like, the best milkshakes ever. They taste like . . ."

Alex kept talking, but I couldn't focus on everything he was saying. Did he just ask me on a date?

"And they top it with this delicious whipped cream and chocolate syrup. It's out of this world! You'll love it!"

"Okay," I said, laughing. I assumed his parents would drive us there, but still, it would be nice to get out of the house for a change.

"I hope this pandemic will end real soon, you know," he said. "I'm not getting any younger."

I burst out laughing. He always cracks me up.

"I gotta go to bed," I said.

"Yeah, me too. Sweet dreams."

I wish I could hang out with my friends like in the old days.

THIS VIRUS SUCKS!

MONDAY

We've been studying ancient civilizations, and my favorite lessons are about Egypt.

Today, Mom taught us about THE MUMMIES!!

She showed us vivid pictures of mummified people who died thousands of years ago in Egypt.

Trust me—she had our full, undivided attention!

"Ancient Egyptians believed in life after death, but only if their bodies were saved. When they mummified the bodies, they cut open the person's chest and removed the organs. The intestines, stomach, liver, and lungs were cleaned and preserved in special canopic jars that were later put into the tomb. The only organ they kept in the body was the heart."

"Why the heart and not the brain?" I asked.

"Ancient Egyptians thought the heart was the soul of a human and not the brain," Mom said. "Because they considered the brain useless in the afterlife, they removed it from the skull by inserting an iron hook up the dead person's nose and pulling it out one gooey piece at a time."

NOW, THIS IS THE TYPE OF LESSON I LOVE!

"Did they preserve the brain in a jar, too?" Natalia asked.

"No, the brain was one of the few organs they threw away."

Natalia and I started laughing.

Man, if they only knew how important the brain is!

Maybe if they kept the brain inside the body, the mummies would have a chance to live like they had expected them to.

Oh well, too late now!

"After the body was filled with natron salt and dried, it was packed with rags, plants, and spices to look like a human body, and then it was wrapped in linen. After priests performed a few religious rituals, the body and the canopic jars were prepared for burial."

"This is so cool!" I said.

"The royal mummies were put in tombs with many objects they may need in the afterlife: jewelry, clothing, food, games, even chariots, and mummified pets. The pyramids were built to serve as tombs for Egyptian rulers."

"Wow! Best lesson ever!" I said.

Mom smiled and asked us to build our own pyramids from cardboard boxes and make our own mummies from empty toilet paper rolls, which we could decorate to resemble us, the way they did in ancient Egypt.

"When you are done," Mom said, "draw the things you would put in your own tomb to help you live in the afterlife, cut the objects out of paper, and put them in your tombs."

We were excited about this project, and we quickly started building our own pyramid, sarcophagus, and mummy.

When we were done, Mom asked what we put inside the tomb for the afterlife.

Unsurprisingly, Natalia put cutout drawings of toys, fancy dresses, food, and water.

I decided on these things in my tomb:

- A cell phone—probably the most important item needed in the afterlife
- My tablet—to play the BUILDING WORLDS game
- A stack of books
- Some clothing, food, and water
- This diary and a pen

Mom sighed when she saw my chosen treasures. "Do you really think the cell phone and the tablet would work in the afterlife?" she asked.

"They'd better have internet in paradise because these items are essential to my existence," I said and smiled.

And if they don't have internet there, I will haunt the living until they do!

OCTOBER

WEDNESDAY

I love playing pranks on my sister.

Mom gets mad at me for doing it, but I don't know how to stop it.

The need to play those jokes is stronger than my will, and I can't do anything about it.

This morning, I did something that got me in trouble, but when you're quarantined in the house for months, it's hard not to get creative with your time.

And by creative, I mean planning pranks.

I don't know where you live, but here in the islands, we have those gigantic cockroaches called PALMETTO BUGS.

They love moist, dark, and humid places, like under the mulch, under pots in the shed, under Mom's gardening tools, and between leaves on the ground.

We all are used to seeing them outside, but NOBODY wants them inside the house.

TRUST ME!

This morning, Mom mentioned the bugs had gotten into her gardening shed again, and I watched her describe them with disgust.

We were eating eggs and sausage for breakfast, but I knew Mom had cooked kidney beans in the fridge for today's lunch, which gave me a great idea for another prank.

When Mom got up from the table and wasn't looking, I whispered to my sister for her to close her eyes, and I explained that I was going to put something in her mouth so she could guess what it was.

She likes playing games, so she closed her eyes and opened her mouth.

I took one large kidney bean from the meal in the fridge and put it on her tongue. She tasted it and then ate it.

"It was a bean," she said, proud of herself.

I shook my head. "No, it wasn't."

"Then what was it?"

"A palmetto bug!" I said, laughing.

Natalia cried immediately, and Mom turned around to see what was happening.

"Sylvia made me eat a cockroach!" my sister screamed.

Mom eyed me in shock. "Sylvia, where did you see a cockroach? In this house? In the kitchen? On the table?"

I laughed because it was funny how Mom worried about cockroaches in the house more than the fact that Natalia might have just eaten one.

I nodded, carrying on with my prank. "Yes, Mom. It was right here on the table."

Natalia was still screaming, but Mom was already busy tearing apart the entire kitchen, looking for cockroaches.

IT WAS ONE BIG MAYHEM!

Dishes were moved to the sink, all cabinet doors were opened, and a broom flew all over the floor.

Mom was holding a KILL ALL BUGS spray with determination on her face—like a superhero, ready to attack the enemy.

😁

I laughed, but then I felt a tiny bit sorry for Mom, so I decided to soften the blow.

"I think it was just this one cockroach, Mom. But you don't have to worry about him because Natalia ate it."

Natalia screamed even louder, tears streaking down her cheeks, which stopped Mom in her tracks.

She grabbed my sister and looked at her as if trying to see if she would transform into a cockroach—or so I imagined.

Mom gave me a stern look. "Did you really make your sister eat a cockroach?"

I decided to continue with my prank because it was kind of funny that everyone believed me.

"Yes," I said, "I made her eat the cockroach. But at least now the bug won't lay eggs in the kitchen, and they won't spread all over the house."

Mom says I always need to look on the bright side, right?

Natalia screamed even louder, which I didn't think was possible.

"To your room, Sylvia. NOW!" Mom yelled. "I will deal with you later!"

When I was sitting in my room, I only waited for the next IMPENDING BOOM.

I knew I would be grounded, but when the whole world is OFF LIMITS, what could Mom forbid me to do that wasn't forbidden already?

After Mom calmed down Natalia and searched the entire house for cockroaches, the door to my room opened, and Mom barged in. "Why would you do such a horrible thing?"

In situations like these, I tend to be completely unresponsive. I stare at the floor and don't know what to say.

😔

I don't know why I do things. I just do.

Mom stared at me, waiting for my defense, but nothing came out of my mouth.

"You are grounded. No cell phone, no games, and no internet for two weeks!" she said and closed the door behind her.

WHAT?? NO!!

😮

This was a nightmare! How was I supposed to function with NOTHING to do?

I came out of my room because I figured if I apologized to my sister, she would tell Mom, and I would be allowed to be on my electronics again.

When I entered Natalia's room, she turned away from me.

"I'm sorry I made you eat the bug," I said.

What? I apologized, didn't I?

Doesn't the apology count? This may be my best prank ever! I'm not ready to fess up yet.

Natalia didn't even look at me and left her room without saying a word.

I guess she isn't talking to me now.

Fine! I don't need my sister!

☹

Actually, I've been getting tired of her being around me for months!

Without seeing other kids, she's been demanding a lot of my attention, so I'm fine being left alone!

We've been stuck together for months during this pandemic, and I can use some isolation around here.

I can't believe I was trying to find the thief who stole her backpack!

Obviously, people around here don't see the bigger picture.

If she doesn't appreciate me, then I'll abort my mission to search for more clues, and she will never find out who took her stuff!

THURSDAY

Everyone is still mad at me.

Natalia refuses to talk to me and treats me like I don't exist.

Mom still searches for cockroaches all over the house, and Dad shows his disappointment with me every time he sees me.

"I thought you were a big girl now. I thought kids don't do silly things in middle school," he said this morning.

"We don't miraculously change just because it's another year, Dad," I responded, but he didn't want to hear it.

I tried to enjoy this unexpected peace away from my sister, who always steals everyone's attention.

I've been looking for things to do, but I am lost without my tablet and my games.

I read a book, but even that got boring for me.

I took out my drawing pad and tried to sketch a few things, but I didn't seem to have any inspiration to do it.

Now I'm bouncing off the walls, and I wish my sister were with me.

I never thought I would admit it, but I miss getting in trouble with her and doing things together.

But she is still giving me the cold shoulder, so I am on my own.

☹

This afternoon, I went outside on my bike, and I circled our street twice.

I rode by Jeremy's house to see whether he was hanging out in his front yard.

And sure enough—there he was!

The only problem was, I didn't know what to say to him AGAIN.

He waved. "Hey!"

"Hi," I answered like an idiot, lost for words, and I skidded to a stop.

"Did you find the thief?" he asked from his front porch.

"Not yet."

He walked down his driveway and stopped ten feet from me, so neither of us had to put on the masks.

"Where do you go to school?" he asked.

"The local island school. But now I'm homeschooled."

"Because of the virus, right?"

"Yes."

"Don't you miss hanging out with other kids? I'm going crazy doing virtual classes at home."

"Did you join our island school?" I asked, crossing my fingers behind my back.

"No, the virtual classes are from a private online school."

"Oh. We have a small local school on the island that is . . . cool." I CAN'T BELIEVE I JUST SAID THAT! COOL? Really? What happened to me during the pandemic?

"Oh, yeah? My mom said I could choose which school to join in the islands when the pandemic is over. But I was thinking about the middle school one hour away from here. It's a bigger building."

I sighed, trying to hide my disappointment. "I used to think a bigger school would be better for me, too, but I like the small island school more. Everyone knows each other, no matter what age. And we have an art classroom with its own pottery studio."

"Interesting. Do you like living in the islands? I'm not used to living in such a small town, away from everything."

I smiled. "At first, I was skeptical. I missed the entertainment a city can offer. But now . . . I do like it. My parents rent vacation homes to tourists, and people from all over the world come here just to experience a week or two of the life we have every day. You can't beat a tropical place with great snorkeling and dolphins everywhere."

Jeremy listened to me like I was describing the latest edition of his favorite game, and I liked the way he looked at me.

"Maybe, one day, you can show me around?" he asked.

I could feel my cheeks burning, and for the first time, I wished I had my face mask on. "Sure. . . ."

"Well, it was nice talking to you. I gotta go."

I waved him goodbye and rode home.

I thought about my afternoon and realized this was probably the longest conversation I had ever had with a stranger in my entire life.

The only boy who could achieve this was Alex, but it took me a month to open up to him.

I had only known Jeremy for a couple of days, but he had already broken down the walls surrounding me for years.

On my way home, I decided to fess up to my prank and ease everyone's mind by telling them the truth.

But when I returned to the house, two utility trucks were parked in front of our home. Strange men were coming in and out of the front door.

As soon as I entered, I asked Mom and Dad what was going on.

Mom sighed. "I am having the house exterminated against bugs right now. I called them yesterday, and they were able to come today."

"WHAT?" I asked, clearly in shock.

"Yes, honey," Dad added. "And I have the plumbers here, checking for any leaks under the sinks, in the walls, or in the storage room because cockroaches love moist places. I'm just trying to figure out how they got into the house."

I was about to faint!

"The sad part is . . ." Mom said, "I had to get rid of all our food from the pantry . . . So, not only have we wasted all that food we stocked up during the pandemic, but we also needed to pay for the exterminator and the plumbers. . . ."

Dad sighed this time. "With our current financial situation, it's terrible timing for such an expense, but at least our house won't get infested with cockroaches."

I was getting weak in my legs, so I went to my room.

THIS CAN'T BE HAPPENING!

I wanted to scream:

IT WAS ONLY A PRANK!!

What do I do now?

I should have told them the truth yesterday. I let it go for too long!

I know Mom is very sensitive about bugs, but I didn't think she would go that far and call an exterminator!

So, now that my parents wasted money because of me, I will be grounded whether or not I confess.

I'm not sure if telling her the truth about the kidney bean will make things any better.

Mom says deception is as bad as doing the wrong thing in the first place.

It's one thing to trick your sister into eating a bug, but it's a completely different situation when things escalate to the point where:

1. An exterminator comes to the house and sprays the entire place.
2. Mom gets rid of food from the pantry.
3. Dad has plumbers looking for leaks all over the house.

I realize things got OUT OF CONTROL, and if I fess up, I may be grounded even longer!

I'm not sure what is worse—denying the truth or saying I'm guilty.

I feel like they have just backed me into a corner, and no matter what I say, it will get me in trouble anyway.

So, I'm doing what I think is best for my survival.

I am keeping quiet. . . .

SATURDAY

I can't believe I'm writing this, but I really miss hanging out with my sister.

I try to engage with Natalia, but she always leaves the room when I enter. She plays with her dolls, paying me no mind.

Unfortunately, it looks like she doesn't want to do anything with me anymore.

In a world where so many things are OFF LIMITS because of the virus, spending time with my sibling is all I've got.

Another thing is, I'm dying without my electronics!

A new version of BUILDING WORLDS came out yesterday, and I can already imagine getting to the next level and building stuff I can't probably describe right now.

So, being grounded from the internet and completely isolated from my friends and sister is getting the worst out of me.

Yesterday, for example, I noticed I started talking to myself.

I don't know what I was talking about because the other part of me wasn't listening.

Then I caught myself turning the night lamp on and off while lying in bed, amused with the technology I DID have access to.

It reminded me of that movie where a guy was stranded on a desert island and had to survive for years with no civilization.

I kind of felt like him—secluded from everyone, with no source of entertainment, starting to look like a caveman, going nuts, and talking to myself.

Before things got even worse, I needed to do something not to lose the remaining sanity I still had (hopefully!).

So, this morning, I kept searching for the thief.

I figured if I found him, my sister and my parents would definitely welcome me back into the family, forgive me for wasting food and money because of my prank, and return my electronics.

I sneaked into Natalia's room and took one of her other pink backpacks.

The reason I use her things to bait the thief and not mine is that someone OBVIOUSLY likes Natalia's taste, and I don't own anything in pink for sure.

I know my head is on the line—if I lose Natalia's backpack like I had lost her beach bag, I may as well pack MY BAGS and leave for good—but I am determined.

I grabbed a few long lollipops from the kitchen, which I stuffed into the outside pockets of the backpack—to attract the PREDATOR.

I added Natalia's miscellaneous toys to the rest of the outside pockets so they would be easily visible from far away. I put more of her toys inside the backpack to make it look full.

Yes, I know—I'm taking her stuff without asking her.

I get it! You don't have to tell me!

But serious situations sometimes involve drastic measures.

☺

While my family was watching a movie, I snuck out of the house and placed the backpack outside of the gate.

I waited behind a bush, my eyes never leaving that backpack.

This time, I had plenty of snacks to carry me through the day.

I wished Mom hadn't taken away my phone as my punishment because I couldn't record the thief in the act anymore.

I just had to confront him myself.

So, I waited. . . .

First, I noticed Jeremy riding on his bicycle.

Great! I looked ridiculous hiding in a bush!

I was hoping he wouldn't see me.

I watched him as he stopped in front of the backpack, and for a moment, I thought he was the one who had stolen my sister's things.

He stared at the backpack for a minute and looked around as if trying to spot someone.

Then he squinted and looked right at me.

I held my breath, hoping to blend in with the leaves, but it didn't work because he approached me, leaned down, and smiled.

"Good hiding spot. Almost invisible," he said.

I felt so embarrassed!

"It's the only bush on the street," I said, which was true.

In fact, that bush is just a bunch of overgrown weeds my dad has never cut off from the front of our property.

Mom asked him to get rid of it several times, but Dad procrastinated because the bush had grown a thick trunk, and now it needs to be professionally removed, stump and all.

He just gives it a trim every week, making sure it won't grow into a tree.

"It's perfect. Just hide your shoes a little bit more," Jeremy said.

I pulled my feet in closer to me. "Wish me good luck."

"So, what's the plan when you catch him?"

I shrugged. "I don't know. I'll figure it out. The most important thing is that I DO catch him."

Jeremy nodded. "Okay, so I'll be riding here close by in case you need my help to tackle the guy. Just shout, okay?"

I laughed. "Okay."

Jeremy took off, and I was once again left on watch.

After about half an hour, I saw what I was looking for!

THE DUDE was riding on his skateboard, and when he passed our property, he noticed the backpack.

I wasn't sure where Jeremy was, but I didn't see him anywhere, which was probably better, as I didn't want to scare away the PREDATOR.

THE DUDE stopped in his tracks, approached the backpack, and laughed while shaking his head. "How can you be so stupid again!"

He left WITHOUT taking anything.

First, I was mad because he was just plain mean. But then I realized he wasn't the one taking my sister's stuff, after all.

I was kind of disappointed because I thought this was it—I would catch him in the act!

Then I realized I was dealing with a completely new person, and I had no suspect.

I was getting a little bit worried now.

What if it was a REAL burglar, someone very dangerous?

How was I supposed to face a real criminal all by myself?

At this point, I really hoped my family would appreciate me risking my life for my sister.

And if anything happened to me, I hoped they would throw a big, fancy funeral for me as they do for heroes or something.

So, I sat there for another hour, quite surprised my family didn't even notice I was gone for so long.

My legs grew restless, and I think some bugs were chewing on my ankles.

I shifted a little so the bugs would leave me alone, then I noticed a strange figure coming down our street.

I sat still, even though I felt tiny things crawling on my legs.

The kid wore a hood over his face, so I couldn't see him clearly. Then he quickly approached the backpack and PICKED IT UP!

As he turned around and started to leave, I jumped out of the bush, yelling, "Got you!"

When I pulled down the hood, I was speechless.

😮

It was **MAX GUNOV!**

The bully from Natalia's class!

Can you believe it?

He looked at me in anger. "Leave me alone," he said, trying to get away from me.

"Leave YOU alone?" I shouted. "You've been stealing from my sister for weeks now, and you want ME to leave YOU alone?"

I grabbed his arm, making sure he wouldn't run away.

Then I saw Jeremy riding by. He stopped.

"Is everything okay?" he asked.

"Yes. Thanks. I found the thief."

Jeremy looked at Max, confused. I bet he was thinking the same thing I was—a boy stealing girly stuff?

"I'm glad. Do you need my help?" Jeremy asked.

"I will be fine, thank you," I said.

If my sister could fight him, so would I!

Jeremy nodded, but he didn't leave. "I will stay just in case." He crossed his arms in front of his chest and looked at Max with a stern look.

I smiled because it was nice to have a good-looking bodyguard by my side.

Then my attention turned toward Max, who was still trying to get away. "Why did you steal those things from my sister? She had all her savings in her first backpack!"

He wasn't talking, so I yelled louder. "Tell me! Why did you steal from my sister?"

"Answer her," Jeremy added.

I heard the front door open at my house, and my whole family was out of the gate now.

"What's going on?" Mom asked.

"I found the thief," I said.

Mom looked at Max and Jeremy, so I needed to clarify.

"This is our new neighbor, Jeremy. He is helping me to confront Max. Max is the one who took Natalia's stuff."

Mom looked at Max and shook her head. "How do you know that?"

"I set up a trap with another backpack, and he was just about to walk away with it!" I pointed to Natalia's backpack, still on Max's shoulder.

"Hey! That's mine!" Natalia screamed.

"Young man," Mom said, approaching Max, "is this true? Have you been taking Natalia's things?"

I don't know why Mom asked that question since the proof was in front of her.

"I found them. Those things were outside of your gate, so they were free to take," he said.

"Did you know they belonged to Natalia?" Dad asked.

Max nodded.

"Then why would you take them? Natalia worked very hard for her money," Mom said.

"Natalia got me in trouble at the grocery store. She knocked down cereal boxes by riding on a shopping cart, and I was blamed for it! I had to clean them up."

Dad looked at Natalia. "Is this true?"

Natalia's face flushed with a red color. "Um, yes... but..."

I JUST LOVE SEEING MY SISTER IN TROUBLE FOR ONCE!

"Natalia, apologize to Max," Dad said.

My sister lowered her head. "I'm sorry...."

Dad stepped closer to Max. "Max, you get yourself in a lot of trouble at school. And now you come here and take Natalia's things. You keep up with this bad behavior, and you will be seriously in trouble with the police."

Max's eyes opened wide. "You aren't gonna call the police on me, right? I'm only a kid!"

Dad crossed his arms. "I have to report the three stealing incidents. Those bags may have been outside of the gate, but they were still on my property."

Max looked like he was about to cry.

"Max, can you please return all of Natalia's things?" Mom asked. "If you do so, we won't call the police."

Max nodded. "Yes." He handed Natalia her backpack. "I'll bring the rest tonight."

Dad cleared his throat. "Anything you should say to Natalia?"

"Sorry for taking your stuff," Max hissed.

"And . . . ?" Dad asked.

Max looked into Natalia's eyes. "Sorry for calling you names at school and pushing you on the playground."

Natalia sighed. "I'm sorry I bit your hand."

Max narrowed his eyes. "I still have a mark from your teeth."

"Why are you on the street all by yourself, Max?" Dad asked him.

"My grandmother lives on the next street, and I've been staying with her during the pandemic. I was riding on my bike when I saw Natalia cleaning someone's window. That's how I knew she lives here."

"All right then, thank you," Mom said.

When Max walked away, Mom turned to Jeremy. "It's nice to meet you, Jeremy. I know your mom. Before the pandemic, we used to go to yoga classes together. She told me you would be moving onto our street. I'm glad you met Sylvia already."

"Nice to meet you all," Jeremy said.

"I'm Natalia," my sister said and grinned from ear to ear, using every bit of her charm she could.

Jeremy nodded and smiled. "Now that the mystery of missing things is solved, I better go. See you later, Sylvia."

My heart skipped a beat. "Thanks for sticking around."

"You did it all on your own," Jeremy said and walked away.

We all headed to our house. Unsurprisingly, I was the new hero.

I told my family how I had planned the setup for days and then had to hide in treacherous conditions outside for hours, facing danger every step of the way.

"You did good, Sylvia," Mom said. "I'd give you back your electronics, but you're still grounded after that stunt with the cockroach."

That's when I knew I had to do the right thing, after all.

I looked at my sister and admitted to my prank. "It wasn't a cockroach. It was just a kidney bean from Mom's meal in the fridge. You were right when you guessed it. I'm sorry."

I think Mom could breathe better after hearing it, but I was waiting for my sister's response.

Natalia laughed, then said, "I knew it was just a bean all along. But I played it as if I believed you so Mom would ground you and take away all your electronics."

WHAT?

Next time, I'll have to UP my game with this kid for sure!

As I suspected, Mom and Dad were not pleased I let the prank go so far that they spent money on an exterminator and plumbers and went crazy for days.

"As your punishment, no cell phone for a month!"

WHAT? NO!

And when Max later returned all Natalia's missing things (including the money!), they still didn't let me off that easily.

Mom served kidney beans for dinner, and I was forced to eat the entire helping on my plate to learn a lesson.

I HATE KIDNEY BEANS!

THURSDAY

I like fall, even though we live on a tropical island, and we technically do not have seasons the way everyone has up North.

The summer heat gives way to a cool breeze, days are shorter, and everyone decorates their homes for Halloween.

This morning, Natalia and I carved pumpkins to decorate our property in front of the gate.

Dad had already finished stringing purple and orange lights on the fence, and Mom hung the fall wreath on the door.

When Natalia and I were outside, putting our pumpkins near the mailbox, we heard someone riding a skateboard behind us.

"Well, well, well . . ." THE DUDE said. "Your pumpkins are missing something, don't you think?"

I rolled my eyes, annoyed to see him. "What are they missing?"

"The PULP!" he said and lifted some kind of bag above our heads.

Within a few seconds, we had orange pumpkin pulp with seeds dripping from our heads and clothes.

"NOOOO!" we both said.

"I saved it just for you, girls!" he said and laughed.

"Payback time!"

We were completely covered in an orange, gooey mess.

I couldn't believe we had gotten cornered like that and fell vulnerable to his attack.

I should have known he was looking for revenge, after all!

"You will regret this, Dude!" I said in an angry voice.

"Oh yeah? What are you gonna do? Tell your mommy?"

"No, idiot! We're not cowards like you!" I said.

THE DUDE attempted to chase us, so we took off.

We sprinted to hide behind cars parked in front of someone's house. We waited until he left and disappeared from our view.

But as soon as we came out of our hiding space, we heard someone behind us.

"Sporting a new fashion today?" Jeremy asked and laughed.

GREAT! JUST GREAT! IT HAD TO BE JEREMY!

I looked like someone had pooped on me, and I had to bump into the most good-looking boy in the neighborhood.

"Very funny," I said.

"I thought we decorate our houses, not ourselves," he added, smiling.

I laughed. "If you don't stop teasing us, some of this gooey mess will end up on you!"

He laughed as well.

On the way to our house, my sister was curious about this new neighbor.

"How did you meet him?" she asked.

"Jeremy moved here a few weeks ago. I met him when I was looking for your backpack."

"Do you have a crush on him?" she asked without hesitation.

Little kids! I tell you, they are nosy!

"No!" I lied.

She studied my face. "I don't believe you. You have a crush on him."

"Okay, I'll admit it. I may have the tiniest crush on Jeremy, but please, don't tell anyone because I'd die if anyone knew about it."

My sister nodded, satisfied with my answer. She loves secrets!

HALLOWEEN

Halloween is one of my favorite days of the year.

I love scary things, so on that day, Mom doesn't cringe when I research, read, and watch creepy stories.

Any other day, Mom doesn't like it. She is scared of horror movies and tells me life is hard enough without the additional stress.

Scary movies fascinate me, which Mom says is scary in itself.

My friends told me about this cool neighborhood on our island where people go the extra mile with their Halloween decorations.

And I don't mean anything kid-friendly!

No, I'm talking about:

- fake, bloody body parts scattered all over front yards
- fake fog rising between houses
- terrifying screams playing on speakers somewhere in the bushes
- heart-stopping mazes with real people pretending to be murdered or trying to scare the heck out of you
- men in masks chasing people with fake chainsaws

All the adults dress up with their kids, so an apocalypse of zombies surrounds you.

Add the darkness that comes after 6:00 p.m. in October, and you are in for a scary good time!

Unfortunately, this year's Halloween will be a total disaster because of that virus.

☹

The adults contemplated what to do about it for a month and decided to set up some restrictions for everyone to follow.

They figured most kids would be in some kind of mask anyway, so they could trick-or-treat if they followed the new rules.

People are still not allowed to congregate, so there won't be any scary mazes or fall festivals.

Knocking on people's doors and handing out candy are not allowed, either.

Anyone who wants to participate in Halloween activities needs to leave a bowl of candy outside of their homes so kids can grab the treats and go.

The owners can sit six feet apart from the bowl and watch the kids trick-or-treating.

No open candy, no baked goods, only sealed packages to be given to kids.

Everyone needs to wear a COVID-19 mask underneath their Halloween masks.

All families need to walk six feet apart from each other.

To me, all these rules just take away any fun I would have during trick-or-treating, but at least they are letting us have something this fall.

After all holidays and events were canceled this year, I'll take anything they give us.

I called Alex, Tracy, and Grace and asked them to meet our family at the entrance to that neighborhood I told you about.

When we all arrived, I was so happy to see my friends.

We were not allowed to be close to each other, and our parents walked apart from the other parents, but we could finally be together.

🙂

Tracy was dressed like a princess, which totally surprised me.

😠

I would expect such a costume from my sister, but not a sixth grader.

It just shows you the pandemic must be messing with her brain.

Alex was dressed like an apocalyptic warrior or something, and he looked really good in his outfit.

"I like your costume very much," I told him.

He smiled. "I think it suits the pandemic. If the world ends, I'd prefer to die in warrior's clothes, fighting till my last breath, instead of dying in my pajamas, scared of a virus."

I laughed. "You're funny."

"I love the way you look tonight, too. I mean . . . the costume."

Predictably, I was dressed as a zombie with fake blood dripping from my mouth and several fake wounds all over my shins and arms.

You would never catch me wearing a princess gown, for sure.

"Thanks," I replied.

Unsurprisingly, my sister attracted a lot of attention with her cute outfit.

She was dressed as a birthday cake, and everyone who passed us complimented her costume.

Alex's sister, Lily, dressed as a wind-up doll.

I could tell Lily and my sister were so excited to see each other after so many months!

Grace wore a clown outfit.

But she wasn't a nice clown from a circus. She was a scary one from horror movies (not that Mom let me see any of those!), which was so cool!

All our parents were dressed up as well.

Tracy's parents matched their costumes to their daughter's—a princess and a prince. (I'm rolling my eyes here.)

Alex's parents dressed as a cowboy and cowgirl, and they looked great together.

My parents?

Are you ready for this?

Mom dressed as a lollipop and Dad as a muffin.

I stayed far away from them the entire night, and trust me, the pandemic had nothing to do with it!

On the way to our first house, we saw Mrs. Butcher, an old lady who lives on our street.

She always gives me the chills when I see her, but today, her long white dress made her look like a ghost, which scared me for sure.

"Cool costume, Mrs. Butcher," I said, looking at her outfit. "What are you supposed to be? The Corpse Bride?"

Mrs. Butcher looked at me with horror in her eyes. "I'm not wearing a costume."

OOPS!

I quickly turned toward the first house, hoping she wouldn't chase me with a stick or something.

It wasn't as fun to collect candy without actually knocking on people's doors, but we made the best out of the situation.

Alex kept telling jokes the entire time, making us laugh hysterically.

"A father and a son are inside their house. The father slips, falls, and breaks his ankle. 'Son, call nine-one-one,' he says. The son yells, 'Nine-one-one! Nine-one-one! Nine-one-one!'"

We laughed.

"Hey, have you guys heard they are working on a vaccine for this virus?" Alex asked.

"I hope so," I said. "I can't wait for this pandemic to be over."

"Me too," Tracy said.

"Let's hope we'll soon be able to hang out together without these masks again," Alex said.

It got dark pretty quickly, so our parents put those glow necklaces on us so they could see us.

With the weird costumes my parents wore, I was happy not to see them!

As I mentioned before, we had to stay six feet apart from each other, so it was a no-brainer that someone would eventually separate from the pack and get lost.

The only problem was that I didn't expect it to be ME!

After two hours of trick-or-treating, I realized I was following the wrong family.

Since everyone wore costumes, I had no idea who these people were or where my friends were.

I tried to spot a lollipop and a muffin walking somewhere, but I didn't see them.

If you have never been lost on Halloween during trick-or-treating in pitch darkness surrounded by zombies and graveyard decorations everywhere, trust me, it's NOT fun!

I was all alone in total darkness, surrounded by monsters!

Yeah, I knew they were just parents, but I wasn't so sure about some of them.

I mean, if you're a real monster, Halloween is the best time to look for a victim because you can approach her in plain sight.

So, all those weird-looking creatures next to me were giving me some serious chills.

😬

I may be in sixth grade, but my nerves are not mature enough to sustain such stress.

I was passing all kinds of creepy creatures.

The graves in people's front yards seemed to have ghosts coming out of them.

I could hear screams around me.

I searched for my phone in my pockets, but then I remembered I was still grounded from electronics.

I don't cry very often, but I felt tears rolling down my cheeks.

My heart was beating like crazy, and I didn't know what to do.

Then I heard it.

The roar of a chainsaw behind me!

I turned around quickly and saw a masked man in overalls coming right at me.

I screamed so loud . . . I think the entire neighborhood heard me.

AAAAAAA!!!!

I had never been so scared in my entire life.

Then I felt someone grab my hand, and when I turned around, I saw it was a skeleton holding me.

I screamed as loud as I could, fearing for my life.

The skeleton laughed. "Don't be scared. He won't hurt you."

Then, I saw the skeleton remove his skull mask, and you'll never guess who it was!

JEREMY!

When I saw him, I felt a huge relief, and I could finally catch my breath.

"I'm so happy it's only you!" I said.

"Only me," he repeated. "Where's your family?"

"I lost them."

"Don't worry," he said. "My mom will call your mom, and we'll take you home safe and sound."

"Thank you. I'm glad I bumped into you," I said, glad my bloody makeup covered my burning cheeks.

His mom reached my mom on the phone and told her they would drive me home after trick-or-treating.

Because our moms already knew each other from the local yoga classes, I was allowed to stay with them.

Mom said my friends were going home anyway.

I was excited to spend the rest of the night with Jeremy, even if we had to stay a few feet apart.

As it turned out, this Halloween wasn't that awful, after all!

:)

When we were walking down the street, he told me something that made me happy for sure.

"I talked to my mom about joining your island school when the pandemic is over, and she agreed," he said.

"Really?" I asked. I couldn't believe it!

"Yes, and do you know what I can't wait for?"

"What?"

"The PE classes. I love sports!"

Ugh! I wish it was anything else but physical education.

:(

But at least we'd be in the same class because all same-grade students attend PE together in our school.

"Cool," I replied. "I can't believe I'm saying this, but I hope schools will open soon."

He smiled. "Right? It took a pandemic to happen for us to beg to be in school again."

I smiled to myself. It's funny how things work out sometimes.

Who knows—maybe PE will be my favorite subject, after all!

NOVEMBER

SUNDAY

You will never believe what happened!

After all that trick-or-treating yesterday, I felt exhausted, as if I had been running all day.

As if!

Mom told me to lie in bed and rest, and I slept for an entire day!

For dinner, she served me chicken noodle soup because she believes chicken noodle soup fixes everything.

And that's when I knew something was wrong!

I couldn't smell or taste the soup at all!

I put more salt and pepper to make it better, praying it was just my mom's cooking.

But it didn't help because nothing had a taste—not the broth, not the chicken, and not the vegetables!

"What's wrong? Don't you like it?" Mom asked.

I looked at her with fear in my eyes. "I can't taste it or smell it."

Everyone at the table stopped eating immediately.

"Oh no! She has COVID!" Mom said and got up from her chair.

She went to the kitchen and returned with an apple and some orange juice in a glass. "Tell me if you can taste them."

I took a bite of the apple, then I shook my head. Nothing.

I took a sip of the orange juice. "I don't taste anything," I said.

She removed a small bottle of perfume from her pocket and sprayed my wrist. "Can you smell it?"

I sniffed my wrist, but I couldn't detect any smell. "No. . . ."

Mom checked my temperature, and I had a fever!

"Oh no! This must be coronavirus for sure!" Mom said.

"Will Sylvia die?" Natalia asked with tears in her eyes.

"No," Mom said, "she will be fine. Kids do better with COVID than adults. But I'm afraid we all need to wear masks around each other from this point on. And Sylvia will need to quarantine in her room all by herself."

"For how long?" I asked.

"Two weeks, I'm afraid."

TWO WEEKS??

"We will take you to the doctor tomorrow," Dad said. "You will need to be tested for COVID."

"With that long swab stick?" I asked, disappointed. "It will touch my brain!"

Natalia giggled. "Like they did it with the mummies— up the nose to remove the brain!"

"Natalia!" Mom said. "This is no time for jokes like that."

I sighed. "She is right ... I will pass out for sure!"

"You will be fine," Mom said and handed us face masks.

After Mom gave me medicine to reduce my fever, I retreated to my room for the night.

I couldn't sleep for a while because I heard Mom disinfecting the entire house.

MONDAY

In the morning, I woke up with a runny nose and a cough, which made me feel even worse than yesterday.

Dad stayed with Natalia at home, and Mom took me to the doctor.

But as soon as we arrived, the lady in the office told us we couldn't wait inside to prevent others from getting COVID from me, even though everyone wore face masks.

All the patients in the waiting room looked at me with fear in their eyes, treating me like I was the deadly infectious disease.

We waited outside for half an hour before a nurse covered like an astronaut came over to take Mom and me inside.

The nurse had a large isolation gown on, gloves, an N95 face mask, goggles, and a plastic shield in front of her face.

When she opened the test kit and removed the long swab stick, I gasped.

😮

She lowered my mask and inserted the swab deep into my nostril, turning it around in circles.

I saw stars right before my eyes.

Then, she took the same swab and inserted it into my other nostril (YUCK!!!), collecting whatever was inside.

The whole time, I prayed my brain was still intact.

After that, the doctor came and did a checkup. He listened to my chest for a long time.

"Do you have difficulties breathing?"

"No."

"Do you have pain in your chest?"

"No."

"Do you have muscle pains?"

"Yes, a little."

"Can you cough for me?"

I coughed.

"Dry cough," he said. "Common for COVID. But I don't see anything alarming right now."

"Do I have coronavirus?" I asked.

"We will know the results in a few days," he said. "In the meantime, treat the sickness like the flu. Use medication to reduce the fever. I will prescribe you a syrup for your cough and runny nose. Take extra vitamins, especially C, D, B, and zinc. And elderberry syrup."

"Thank you, Doctor," Mom said.

"She should quarantine for fourteen days. I will call you as soon as the results are in," the doctor said and turned toward me. "Take care of yourself. You'll be fine. Call me if you are not getting better. And come back in two weeks so we can test you again."

"Again?" I said, disappointed.

😩

The doctor nodded and smiled. "You want to return to society, don't you? We need to make sure you are no longer infectious."

"We will, Doctor," Mom said.

After we left the doctor's office, Mom stopped at the pharmacy while I waited in the car to prevent the virus from spreading.

When we returned home, I took vitamins and my medication and went to my room, where I stayed all day, watching movies and reading books.

Occasionally, Mom entered the room with a tray full of food, but none of the meals made me feel better.

I still couldn't taste anything.

TUESDAY

"You should notify your friends about your sickness to make sure they don't have it," Mom said this morning. "You probably got COVID during trick-or-treating on Halloween."

"You are right," I said.

Soon, I connected with Alex, Tracy, and Grace online, where we could see each other.

I told them I probably had COVID, and I was waiting for the test results.

My friends felt sorry for me and wanted to know how it felt to have coronavirus. None of them had any symptoms, and they all felt fine.

I told them about my fatigue, cough, runny nose, fever, and the lack of smell and taste.

"If none of us have it, then how did you get the virus?" Tracy asked.

"I don't know! When I got lost, I bumped into my neighbor, and he took me home. Other than him, I only was close to you guys."

"We were wondering what happened to you," Grace said. "Alex wanted to search the entire neighborhood for you."

☺

"Aww..." I said. "That's sweet."

"I would have," Alex said, "if your mom didn't say you left with someone else."

"I'm sorry. I didn't mean to abandon you guys. I was genuinely lost."

"We forgive you this time," Alex said. "But next Halloween, I will put twenty glow stick necklaces on you and reflective tape on your back."

We all burst out laughing.

"I miss you guys already!" I said. "Let's hope this pandemic ends soon, and we all can return to school and hang out."

My friends wished me a quick recovery from COVID, and we ended our online meeting.

Next, I wondered how I would contact Jeremy.

Then I came up with a plan.

I scribbled down a note:

> Jeremy,
>
> I really enjoyed spending some time with you on Halloween. Thank you for the ride home.
>
> Unfortunately, I've been sick since Sunday. Probably COVID. Waiting on test results.
>
> Hope you are well and feel okay.
>
> If you need to reach me, don't hesitate to call me at this number: 555-0173.
>
> Sylvia

Did you notice how I politely and nonchalantly provided my cell phone number?

I asked my sister to meet me on the other side of my door. I didn't want her to get coronavirus, but I needed her help.

"What's going on?" I heard her voice behind the closed door.

"Can you do something for me? Could you bring a note to Jeremy?"

"Sure."

"Thank you. I am sliding it under the door," I said and explained to her which house belonged to him.

Then I crossed my fingers, hoping he would contact me soon.

Half an hour later, I received a text message from Jeremy.

Hey, neighbor. Thank you for the note.

The corners of my mouth lifted in excitement because I finally had his phone number, too!

Hi. You're welcome.

Geez, really? That was my answer? Couldn't I say something more exciting? Like "Anything for you!"

OMG, I'm glad I wasn't stupid enough to write that!

Can you imagine? Anything for you. So lame!

J: I owe you an apology.

S: For what?

J: I'm afraid you got COVID from me.

S: Oh, no! Are you sick, too?

J: Yes! I was hoping you didn't catch it. If I knew I had coronavirus, I would have stayed far away from you.

S: That's okay. I prefer your germs to some stranger's. Besides, you rescued my life.

J: And then I gave you COVID.

S: Hahahaha . . . True.

J: I will need to pay you back for your sacrifice.

S: Hahaha . . . What do you have in mind?

J: Since we will both be immune to coronavirus when we recover, we could finally hang out without the fear of getting the virus, right?

S: Right!

J: So, how about I take you for pizza, and you show me your school, so I know where I'm going when they finally end virtual classes?

S: I would like that!

J: Then it's a plan! Get better soon, neighbor.

S: You too!

I can't believe I made a friend during the pandemic lockdown!

I'm looking forward to introducing Jeremy to Alex when we all return to school.

Of course, I'm not planning to tell Alex I have a crush on my new neighbor. I just want them to become friends and get along well.

What could possibly go wrong this time, right?

MONDAY

My test results came back positive, which means I definitely have CORONAVIRUS.

So far, my family is doing well, and nobody besides me has any symptoms.

I spend my days in my room, doing online classes, reading books, and texting with all my friends.

I still can't taste or smell my food, which makes eating difficult.

But after a week of quarantine, I feel like I'm going crazy!

Mom lets me be outside on the swings, on the trampoline, or in the pool as long as I am away from Natalia.

Which sucks. I kind of miss hanging out with my sister.

I admit that during the pandemic, I begged for my personal space, away from everyone.

I definitely got what I wanted, and I hate it!

I never imagined how lonely I would be without my family around!

This evening, I watched the *Cast Away* movie with Tom Hanks again because I feel like I have something in common with the actor—we are both isolated from the entire world, stuck on an island.

The actor made a face on a volleyball just so he could talk to someone. He got very attached to his Wilson.

And since Dad knows I love this movie, he bought me a volleyball and red paint so I could make my own Wilson and have someone to talk to as well.

SATURDAY

After two weeks of quarantine and a negative COVID test, I am finally free to leave my room and get back to society!

I knew I was getting better as soon as my sense of taste and smell came back, and my cough disappeared.

I must have done a great job isolating myself because nobody from my family got COVID.

But that's not everything!

Today, Mom and Dad told us the good news!

Pharmaceutical companies created a few different vaccines against CORONAVIRUS, and mass production has already started.

"Girls, soon you will be able to return to school in person!" Mom said.

"I cannot believe life will go back to normal!!" I said with joy in my voice.

Do I even remember what NORMAL is?

"And now that the vaccine will be available to everyone, our rental business will do better because people are dying to go on a vacation!"

To celebrate, we decided to have a family day outdoors. We drove to our favorite oceanfront park to spend a day at the beach.

This place is in the center of the island chain, surrounded by beautiful azure waters.

We love coming here because there is a convenience store where you can order lunch, and they have the best ice cream in the area.

😋

When you forget something, which happens to us all the time, the store has everything you need, from beach towels to beach toys and sunscreens to first aid kits.

Mom doesn't like to pack lunches and tons of things just to go to the beach, so she likes the convenience of the store and a clean bathroom and showers on-site.

Besides, the ladies who work there are very nice, and we like hanging out around the store.

The beach in the park is not as crowded as it is on some beaches in the world. We usually find a secluded spot away from everyone—another reason Mom likes it there, especially during the pandemic.

Because the park is on an island, it is connected to a highway with a concrete bridge. There is also another massive, old bridge that used to be a railroad in the past.

Now, broken and dilapidated, it stands as a landmark, reminding us of old times.

People like visiting this area because of the turquoise waters, great snorkeling, and the iconic old bridge.

But when I see the bridge, all I remember is what Dad told Natalia and me about the sharks loving the strong currents that bring plenty of smaller fish to catch.

So now, when I'm on the beach, I think: "bridge = sharks = danger!"

The other day, Dad bought us small kayaks for kids, so we brought them to the beach today.

While Mom and Dad were setting up beach chairs and umbrellas on the sand, Natalia and I pushed the kayaks into the water and went on a ride.

We had fun paddling for about five minutes until our parents screamed from the beach, "Come back!"

I wasn't sure why they were calling for us so frantically, but I told Natalia to turn around and head toward the beach.

And that's where the trouble started.

No matter how much we tried to paddle in our parents' direction, we kept going sideways and farther away.

"What's happening?" Natalia screamed from her kayak.

I looked around and saw what I feared the most—we were drifting toward the old bridge, which is a massive, concrete-and-steel structure with falling debris all around.

Signs all over the bridge warn you to stay away.

The colossal highway-looking bridge may look great in pictures, but it's the last place you want to hang around because of its dilapidating condition.

"The strong current is taking us toward the bridge!" I screamed to my sister, who was about ten feet away from me.

"Not the bridge!" Natalia cried.

I knew what she was thinking. We were in shark-infested waters.

😬

I looked toward my parents, but we were too far away to recognize people on the beach at that point.

We were alone, and Dad didn't have his boat with him.

If we fell out of our kayaks, we would have no chance of survival.

The current was too strong for us to swim—we would drift away out into the sea with nothing to hold on to.

Neither of us could swim for that long.

We were stupid not to put on our vests. We had thought we were on the beach, in two-feet deep water. None of us felt we were in danger of drowning.

But even if we had our vests on, I don't know how long we would float before sharks became interested in us.

If Mom had seen us push the kayaks into the water, she would have made us put on the vests. But we went without them even knowing this, and now we would pay the ultimate price—our lives.

☹

I looked at Natalia, who was already crying.

I couldn't let anything happen to her. No matter how much we argued at times, I couldn't imagine my life without my sister.

"Natalia!" I screamed to catch her attention. "When I come closer, hand me the other end of your paddle. Hold on to it. We will stay together."

She nodded.

I paddled toward her as fast as I could. I wasn't going against the current; we were both floating in the same direction. But I inched sideways toward her and grabbed her paddle.

"Don't let go! No matter what, don't let go!" I said.

She had tears streaming down her cheeks. "I'm scared."

"I know you are. Listen to me, we can't move. If we stay still and together, we will be safe. We won't fall into the water. We will peacefully float until someone rescues us."

"Okay," she said with a trembling voice.

And that's what we did. We held our breath while we were passing the bridge.

The dark shadow of the monster structure loomed over us, and we tried not to imagine the sharks circling underneath our kayaks.

☹

As soon as we passed it, we started drifting out into the open sea.

😬

I saw people on the other side of the beach running, but I knew if I moved my hands in frantic motions, we could fall into the water or separate.

And I DIDN'T want to separate from my sister. I wanted to hold on to her forever!

We were moving farther away from land, and I only prayed we would spot someone on a boat nearby.

"Look!" my sister yelled. "An island!"

I looked in the direction she was pointing, and, as a matter of fact, there was an island.

A small desert island in the middle of nowhere. It had shallow turquoise waters around it, and the current was taking us that way.

I had to think quickly. Do we separate from each other and try to paddle toward the island?

What if we don't make it? What if only one of us reaches the land, and the other one drifts into nowhere all by herself?

I couldn't take that risk.

But I surely didn't want to float any farther away, either.

I pulled my sister's kayak closer to me. "Hold on to my kayak. You can't let go! I will try to paddle us to that island."

My sister nodded with fear in her eyes.

She held on tight to my kayak while I slowly inched toward the island.

I wasn't dealing with rough waters, and at that point, the current wasn't as strong as it was near the bridge.

"Jump into the water!" I said and hopped over the kayak.

"What?" my sister asked, stunned.

"Come on, it's shallow here. Jump before you float away!" I said, holding on to her kayak for dear life.

As soon as she landed near me, we dragged the empty kayaks onto the sand.

We stood on the smallest island I had ever seen, maybe fifty feet across in all directions, surrounded by water.

Only one palm tree and some weird-looking bushes grew on it.

This whole situation reminded me of the *Cast Away* movie. The man had to survive on a desert island for years, eating coconuts, drinking coconut water, and catching his own fish with a stick.

Now WE were the castaways.

😫

Natalia held on to my hand the entire time we walked around the island. It took us only a minute to circle it completely.

"Only five coconuts hang on that palm tree," I said. "If we each eat one a day, we are good for two days. And that's if I can crack them open with no tools."

"The actor crashed the coconuts on a rock, remember?"

"At first, but then he realized he was wasting the coconut water, so we can't do that. We need to crack open only the top."

Natalia plopped herself down onto the sand. "We're gonna starve!" she cried.

"Don't think like that," I said. "You can try to catch fish as Dad taught you, and I'm good at crushing things."

We burst out laughing.

"I can't eat raw fish," she said.

"I'll make fire just like the actor did. All I need is a few sticks, direct sun, and a breeze underneath the sticks so the fire can breathe, remember?"

"Yeah . . . I think we have a good breeze here."

I couldn't believe that watching that movie with my dad would save my life one day.

And being grounded from electronics would prepare me for real life.

And studying the cavemen showed me how to use stones for tools.

But there I was, trying to survive in the wild.

And what's worse, the pandemic had nothing to do with it!

I had only myself to blame!

Now I was responsible for my sister, and I would not let anything happen to her.

No matter what, I would protect her!

I grabbed a rock from the ground and started throwing it at the palm tree so the coconuts would fall down.

Natalia found a stick and started looking for fish in the water.

At some point, we both looked at each other and started laughing.

We laughed so hard that we stopped what we were doing and collapsed on the sand.

Without any fish or coconuts.

I don't know what we would have done if we hadn't heard the roar of an engine on the other side of the island.

We quickly rushed toward it and saw a Coast Guard boat throwing an anchor.

"They came to rescue us!" I said. "We are HEROES!!"

My sister giggled. "We will be famous!"

"They will have a welcome party for us! They will have a TV crew waiting for us, and they will interview us on live TV!"

Natalia clapped. "How do I look?"

"Seriously? You can't look good after what we've been through. We need to ruffle our hair, put mud on our faces, and look dehydrated. That's what they want to see!" I explained.

And that's what we did.

We messed up each other's hair, smeared wet sand on our faces, and walked toward the Coast Guard with our mouths open, dying of thirst.

I know we were dramatizing it a little bit, but that's what you do when you become a famous star.

"Are you girls okay?" a man in a uniform, standing on the beach, asked us. "You are safe now. Come on the boat."

We let them pull us on board, then they grabbed our kayaks.

They gave us water and covered us with blankets.

I sighed. "We are ready to answer all the questions," I said, pretending to be in pain, gasping for air. "We are just happy to see human beings after such a long time...."

The officer looked at me, puzzled. "I was notified you went missing only an hour ago."

Obviously, this guy had no clue what sold on TV these days.

But I wasn't going to let him diminish my chances of becoming a famous star, so I played along with my original plan.

"We had no water and no food with us. We thought we were going to die...." I said, groaning.

"You will see your parents in a few minutes," the officer responded.

And sure enough, we could already see Mom and Dad waiting for us on the dock at the park.

As soon as the boat approached the dock, we ran into our parents' open arms.

"Mom! Dad!" Natalia screamed with joy.

It was the first time I didn't mind hugging my whole family.

I was just so happy to be alive, have my sister by my side, and see my parents again!

"Girls!" Dad said. "You were not supposed to take your kayaks on the bridge side! They don't allow kayaks there because of the swimmers and the strong current! You can use kayaks only on the other side of the beach. Why wouldn't you wait for us to take you?"

"We were just playing around with them. We didn't mean to go anywhere...." I said.

Mom kissed both of us on the cheeks. "I'm so happy nothing happened to you!"

"Um... Mom, Dad, where is the TV crew?" I asked.

"What TV crew?" Mom asked.

"The one to report about our bravery... you know... a missing children story on national TV for the evening news?"

"We didn't notify the news," she said.

"WHAT? YOU DIDN'T CALL THE NEWS? Mom! We could have been on TV!"

"And I don't see a welcome party, either," Natalia said in a sad voice.

"Girls," Mom said, "we are blessed you are safe and sound, but being on TV and a welcome party would be rewarding you for something you did wrong. You should have never taken those kayaks without us knowing and, what's worse, without the vests! As a punishment, no electronics for two weeks!"

"NOOOO!!!" we said in tandem.

With the way things are going for me, all my electronics will be obsolete by the time I get them back.

Just like with the old cassettes and diskettes, when I am finally allowed to use my electronics again, I will look at them and wonder, "What in the world are those?"

But to be honest with you, I'm not that particularly upset about losing my gadgets.

After what I went through today, I'm just happy:

- to be alive
- to have plenty of food
- to have access to fresh water whenever I need it
- to have a bed and a roof to sleep under
- to have my sister

On the way to our spot on the beach, I grabbed Natalia's hand. "I don't know what I would do if something happened to you today."

"You were very brave, Sylvia," my sister said and squeezed my hand. "I was so scared, but you knew what to do."

"All I knew was I had to keep you safe."

My sister looked me in the eye. "I'm so glad YOU are my sister!"

I smiled, but before I could respond, a crowd of strange kids ran toward us.

We were not sure what was happening when they all surrounded us.

"You're survivors!"
"You were so brave!"
"Tell us all about your adventure!"
"Did you see any sharks?"
"Can we have your autographs?"

Natalia and I looked at each other and burst out laughing. We couldn't believe that we had all this attention.

We immediately told a story about how we trudged through rough waters, were taken by the current into shark-infested waters, fought the predators with our paddles, landed on a desert island, and had to survive with no water, no food, and NO CIVILIZATION!! (Well, you get the picture.)

Maybe we didn't end up on national news or get famous, but we are certainly known in our local community now!

And, I'll tell you what, I will take whatever I can get!

THE END

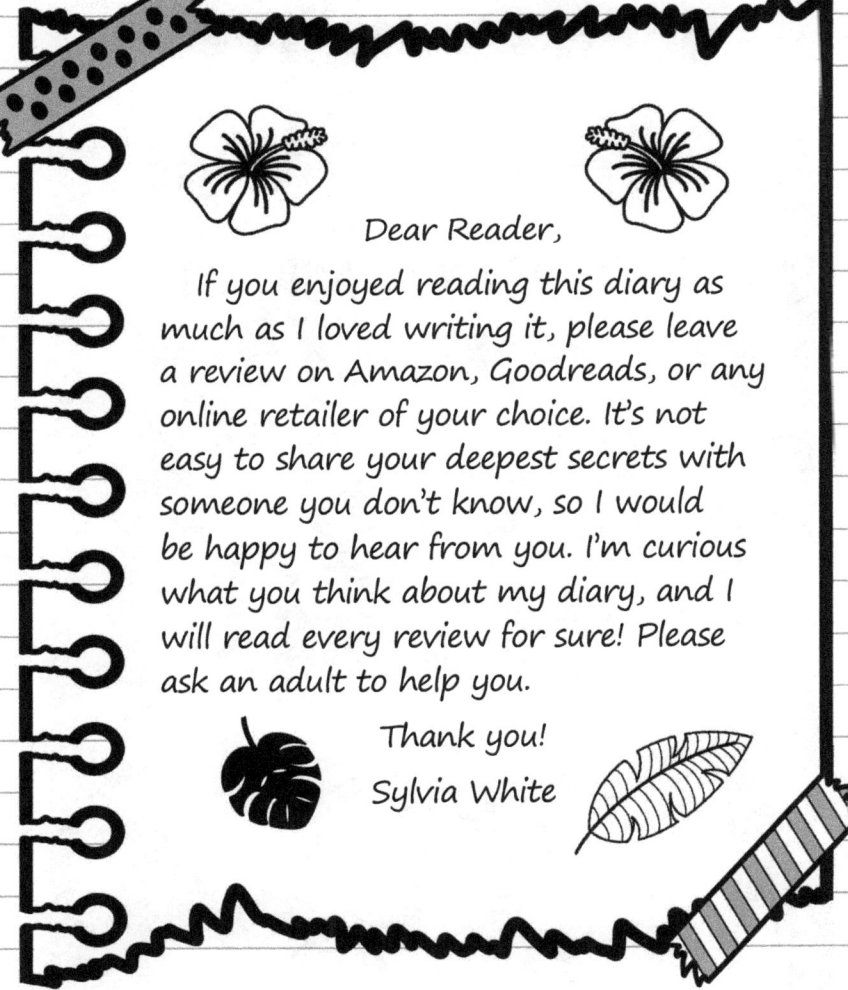

Dear Reader,

If you enjoyed reading this diary as much as I loved writing it, please leave a review on Amazon, Goodreads, or any online retailer of your choice. It's not easy to share your deepest secrets with someone you don't know, so I would be happy to hear from you. I'm curious what you think about my diary, and I will read every review for sure! Please ask an adult to help you.

Thank you!

Sylvia White

ALSO AVAILABLE
MISHAPS IN PARADISE: DIARY OF AN ISLAND GIRL
BOOK 1

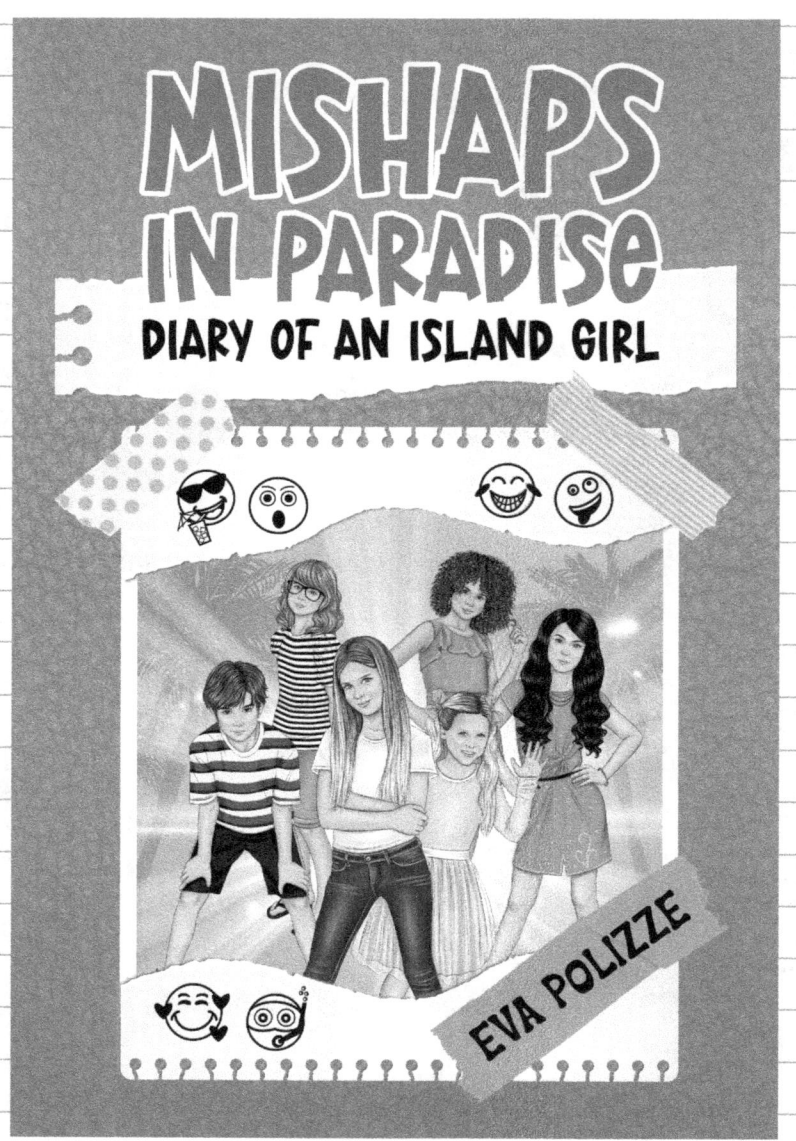

ORDER ONLINE OR AT YOUR LOCAL BOOKSTORE.

FROM THE AUTHOR

Since the day my family and I moved to a tropical island, I knew I wanted to write novels set in the beautiful paradise where I live.

Many stories from *The Pandemic* were inspired by events that happened in real life.

I will never forget March 2020, when the REAL pandemic started. Coronavirus, aka COVID-19, which originated in China at the end of 2019, spread worldwide, killing so many people in its path.

Schools around the world closed down, many businesses shut down, and all events were canceled. People rushed to stores to stock up on food, leaving empty shelves behind for months. Many stores in the States ran out of toilet paper, and its supply was limited to one package per shopper for weeks.

People were not allowed to congregate, always keeping six feet away from one another. Soon, mass production of face masks began, and by the summer of 2020, people all over the world could not leave their homes without them.

When schools closed down at the beginning of the pandemic, kids started virtual learning, struggling to learn online, away from their peers. In the US, many families decided to homeschool to allow their children to be outside during those challenging times.

The pandemic lasted two years. But I decided to end this book in November 2020 because that's when we learned about the creation of the vaccines against coronavirus, when hope for the pandemic to end was high, and when many schools started to open up.

Although the Mishaps in Paradise diaries are fictional stories, they are inspired by my childhood and my two daughters, Olivia and Claudia.

Olivia is three years older and more reserved than Claudia, who is a social butterfly in our family.

We homeschooled for two and a half years, and then my daughters returned to school, happy to see their friends again.

During that time, we enjoyed learning together and exploring the world outside. We had tons of books delivered to our house, and Henry, the skeleton, stood guard in our "classroom," where posters with important information hung on the walls.

This is how Olivia reacted when tons of books were delivered to our house.

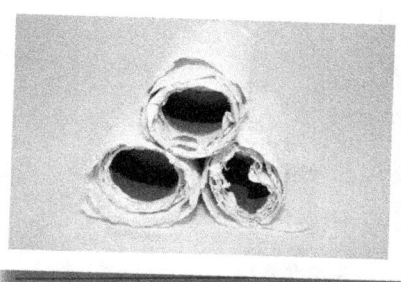

The girls love opportunities to earn their own money. In the early months of the pandemic, my daughters started making toilet paper with their crinkled drawings, happy to give them away for tips.

RV living and traveling can be fun, but it's not for everyone. We experienced all the problems Sylvia writes about staying in the camper.

The backpack story is also true. One day, Claudia decided she wanted to make money on her own and went to our friendly neighbor to clean her window. She earned her first five dollars this way.

Unfortunately, she left her backpack with cleaning supplies and the jar with all her savings in front of our gate (if I only knew why . . .), and it was gone within minutes. Although we searched and asked everyone, we never found her backpack and money. That's when the girls learned about banking and started putting their savings in bank accounts.

When I was a kid, I used to get in trouble a lot. I remember how one day, I covered myself completely in mud (so I wouldn't be recognizable), and I smeared the mess all over my neighbor's door (I'm so sorry!!). Today, I know there are better ways to resolve conflicts.

I also fed my friend a kidney bean and tricked her into thinking it was a cockroach. She never ate beans after that.

The kayak story is based on a similar event that happened to the girls and their friend. They took kayaks into the water unnoticed, were carried by the current, and had to be rescued just before they reached a tiny desert island.

The fishing story is also true. Here is the photo of Claudia with the mangrove snapper. We often see barracudas, baby hammerhead sharks, and tarpons. Sharks are a common sight when we fish.

We also like snorkeling, and the girls explore the local coral reef, where an abundance of colorful fish call it home. While swimming, the girls also see barracudas, small sharks, stingrays, jellyfish, and goliath groupers.

Thank you for reading the Mishaps in Paradise diaries, and I hope you will enjoy the rest of the series. —Eva Polizze

ACKNOWLEDGMENTS

The Mishaps in Paradise books would not have happened without the help of many incredible people.

I would like to thank my two daughters, Olivia and Claudia, for their patience, understanding, and love while I was writing this book. Now you know what it takes to achieve your dreams.

To my husband, Anthony, for his love and support in times he missed me the most. I would have never accomplished my dream without you.

Many thanks to my editor, Jennifer Rees, for helping me shape the Mishaps in Paradise series into the best version possible.

To Brian Paone for the edits and comments on the first draft.

To Emily Fritz for her long hours putting my vision of this book into a reality. I'm looking forward to our next book in the series.

To Kateryna Koralova for the stunning illustrations of the characters. They look amazing!

To Goran Tovilovic for designing the beautiful covers for the series.

To my proofreader, Tiffany Perry, for her insightful comments. I am lucky to have you on my team!

And to all the readers who enjoy the Mishaps in Paradise books. Thank you for your support!

ABOUT THE AUTHOR

Eva Polizze has been drawn to islands since she was a little kid. When she was fifteen, she attended a summer camp in Spain, where she fell in love with palm trees and warm climate regions for life.

When she was seventeen, she won first place in a national writing competition and was awarded a trip to Italy and a three-week vacation in Corsica. After that, she knew she would always be a writer and an island girl.

Over the years, she has traveled to many tropical places in the world, but her dream to live in the islands finally came true when she moved to the Florida Keys in 2014, a place she will always call home. Living on a small tropical island, surrounded by turquoise waters, jumping dolphins, and friendly Key deer, she writes about the island life in her books.

Eva Polizze is the author of the Mishaps in Paradise diaries, a middle school series about two sisters experiencing humorous misadventures on a tropical island. She has two daughters, Olivia and Claudia, who are her inspiration for the books.

You can visit her website at www.evapolizze.com

Find Eva Polizze on:

Printed in the USA
CPSIA information can be obtained
at www.ICGtesting.com
LVHW042054261023
762248LV00003B/38